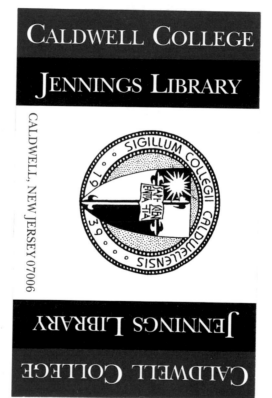

AMERICAN
SOCIAL
MOVEMENTS

THE WHITE
SEPARATIST
MOVEMENT

Mary E. Williams, *Book Editor*

Daniel Leone, *President*
Bonnie Szumski, *Publisher*
Scott Barbour, *Managing Editor*
Stuart B. Miller, *Series Editor*

GREENHAVEN PRESS
SAN DIEGO, CALIFORNIA

THOMSON
──────✶──────™
GALE

Detroit • New York • San Diego • San Francisco
Boston • New Haven, Conn. • Waterville, Maine
London • Munich

Every effort has been made to trace the owners of copyrighted material. The articles in this volume may have been edited for content, length, and/or reading level. The titles have been changed to enhance the editorial purpose.

No part of this book may be reproduced or used in any form or by any means, electrical, mechanical, or otherwise, including, but not limited to, photocopy, recording, or any information storage and retrieval system, without prior permission from the publisher.

Library of Congress Cataloging-in-Publication Data

The white separatist movement / Mary E. Williams, book editor.
    p. cm. — (American social movements)
    Includes bibliographical references and index.
    ISBN 0-7377-1054-3 (hardback : alk. paper) —
ISBN 0-7377-1053-5 (pbk. : alk. paper)
    1. Whites—Race identity—United States—Juvenile literature.
2. United States—History—Autonomy and independence
movements—Juvenile literature. 3. White supremacy
movements—United States—Juvenile literature. 4. United
States—Race relations—Juvenile literature. [1. White supremacy
movements. 2. Racism. 3. Race relations. 4. Hate groups.] I. Title.
II. Series.

E184.A1 W47 2002
305.8'034073—dc21   2001008360

279220

Cover photo: © Mark Richards/PhotoEdit/PictureQuest

CONTENTS

Chapter 1 • THE ORIGINAL KU KLUX KLAN

A Historical Overview of the First Ku Klux Klan
by Paul J. Gillette and Eugene Tillinger
> The Klan may have begun as a form of mischief, but it eventually drew men who had been members of terrorist groups before the Civil War. These men committed unspeakable atrocities against African Americans even after the Klan was officially disbanded.

The Beginnings of the Klan
by Susan Lawrence Davis
> Six Confederate soldiers started the Ku Klux Klan as a form of light diversion. They soon discovered that their costumed night rides frightened blacks and white carpetbaggers and saw their activities as "a way to protect the lives and property of the people of the stricken South."

An Interview with General Nathan Bedford Forrest
by Nathan Bedford Forrest, interviewed by Anonymous
> The first Grand Wizard of the Klan publicly denies his membership in the group—in keeping with the Klan's oath of secrecy—but praises it as a law-abiding, protective military organization. He also discusses his opposition to black suffrage and federal postwar policies.

Chapter 2 • THE EARLY TWENTIETH CENTURY KLAN

Chapter 3 • WHITE SEPARATIST MOVEMENTS OF THE MID–TWENTIETH CENTURY

Chapter 4 • WHITE SEPARATIST MOVEMENTS OF THE LATE TWENTIETH CENTURY

nonwhites are soulless beings created before Adam
and that Jews are the offspring that resulted from
Eve's "original sin" of mating with a nonwhite.

Chapter 5 • PERSONAL NARRATIVES AND PERSPECTIVES ON WHITE SEPARATISM

FOREWORD

H istorians Gary T. Marx and Douglas McAdam define a
social movement as "organized efforts to promote or resist change in society that rely, at least in part, on noninstitu-
tionalized forms of political action." Examining American social movements broadens and vitalizes the study of history by
allowing students to observe the efforts of ordinary individuals and groups to oppose the established values of their era, often in unconventional ways. The civil rights movement of the
twentieth century, for example, began as an effort to challenge
legalized racial segregation and garner social and political rights
for African Americans. Several grassroots organizations—
groups of ordinary citizens committed to social activism—
came together to organize boycotts, sit-ins, voter registration
drives, and demonstrations to counteract racial discrimination.
Initially, the movement faced massive opposition from white
citizens, who had long been accustomed to the social standards
that required the separation of the races in almost all areas of
life. But the movement's consistent use of an innovative form
of protest—nonviolent direct action—eventually aroused the
public conscience, which in turn paved the way for major legislative victories such as the Civil Rights Act of 1964 and the
Voting Rights Act of 1965. Examining the civil rights movement reveals how ordinary people can use nonstandard political strategies to change society.

Investigating the style, tactics, personalities, and ideologies
of American social movements also encourages students to
learn about aspects of history and culture that may receive
scant attention in textbooks. As scholar Eric Foner notes,
American history "has been constructed not only in congressional debates and political treatises, but also on plantations and
picket lines, in parlors and bedrooms. Frederick Douglass, Eugene V. Debs, and Margaret Sanger . . . are its architects as well
as Thomas Jefferson and Abraham Lincoln." While not all

American social movements garner popular support or lead to epoch-changing legislation, they each offer their own unique insight into a young democracy's political dialogue.

Each book in Greenhaven's American Social Movements series allows readers to follow the general progression of a particular social movement—examining its historical roots and beginnings in earlier chapters and relatively recent and contemporary information (or even the movement's demise) in later chapters. With the incorporation of both primary and secondary sources, as well as writings by both supporters and critics of the movement, each anthology provides an engaging panoramic view of its subject. Selections include a variety of readings, such as book excerpts, newspaper articles, speeches, manifestos, literary essays, interviews, and personal narratives. The editors of each volume aim to include the voices of movement leaders and participants as well as the opinions of historians, social analysts, and individuals who have been affected by the movement. This comprehensive approach gives students the opportunity to view these movements both as participants have experienced them and as historians and critics have interpreted them.

Every volume in the American Social Movements series includes an introductory essay that presents a broad historical overview of the movement in question. The annotated table of contents and comprehensive index help readers quickly locate material of interest. Each selection is preceded by an introductory paragraph that summarizes the article's content and provides historical context when necessary. Several other research aids are also present, including brief excerpts of supplementary material, a chronology of major events pertaining to the movement, and an accessible bibliography.

The Greenhaven Press American Social Movements series offers readers an informative introduction to some of the most fascinating groups and ideas in American history. The contents of each anthology provide a valuable resource for general readers as well as for enthusiasts of American political science, history, and culture.

An Overview of the White Separatist Movement

White separatism encompasses a wide assortment of organizations and is not really a single movement, although certain social conditions—particularly an economic upheaval and a perceived change in the balance of power between whites and minorities—seem to spur the growth of such groups. White separatists are often referred to as white supremacists or hate group members because they are depicted as believing that the white race is superior to all others and that whites should exercise violence to dominate minorities. Although many separatists subscribe to these opinions, not all do. As researchers Betty A. Dobratz and Stephanie Shanks-Meile explain in their book *White Power, White Pride!* "Some [separatists] tend to see themselves as . . . advocating the need for whites to assert or regain their power in an America that has become too multicultural. . . . [Others] want the races to be separate, and some of these would seek to achieve this by creating a separate white nation." There are even separatists who claim that each racial group should work to maintain its own culture, without one dominating the other. What all such groups share, however, is the belief in racial separation.

Although the post–Civil War Ku Klux Klan is generally considered America's first white separatist organization, similar race-based vigilante groups existed as early as the 1700s. These groups were organized to capture runaway slaves, thwart slave rebellions, or quell antislavery sentiments among whites. Many communities, for example, established patrol systems wherein mounted guards would monitor roadways and slave quarters to prevent unauthorized travel and assemblies among blacks. After dark, slave patrollers occasionally disguised themselves as ghosts with the intention of frightening blacks and discouraging them from attending nighttime gatherings. Some Southern statutes also allowed patrol leaders to call together a militia to capture groups of fugitives or to suppress potential slave revolts.

During the 1840s and 1850s several secret organizations arose in reaction to the spread of abolitionist attitudes. Groups such as the Knights of the Golden Circle, the Minute Men, and the Knights of the Columbian Order declared an underground war against the so-called enemies of Southern rights. These men would roam the countryside beating, torturing, and sometimes killing people suspected of promoting anti-slavery views. "Persons caught distributing anti-slavery pamphlets or otherwise overtly aiding the abolitionist cause were invariably visited by one or more of these groups," explain journalists Paul J. Gillette and Eugene Tillinger in their 1965 book, *Inside the Ku Klux Klan*. By the early 1860s there were "literally hundreds of cases where men were hanged by mobs simply because they had expressed sentiments not hostile to the United (as opposed to the Confederate) States."

Many historians maintain that the existence of slave patrols and antiabolitionist terrorist groups prior to the Civil War provided fertile ground for the growth of organizations such as the Ku Klux Klan.

THE FIRST KU KLUX KLAN

In late December 1865, six former Confederate soldiers met in a small brick office building in Pulaski, Tennessee, to form a social club for their own amusement. More in the spirit of mischief than of deliberate threat, the "Pulaski Circle" began to parade around at night on horseback bedecked in sheets and pillow cases. The costumed fraternity's nighttime pranks aroused curiosity, and other local men were quick to join. Eventually the group changed its name, adopting *Ku Klux* as an altered version of *kuklos*, the Greek word for "circle," then later adding *Klan* for alliterative purposes.

The Pulaski Klan soon discovered that its activities were particularly intimidating to former slaves, many of whom reportedly took the night riders for ghosts of the Confederate dead. The Klan's "pranks" then came to be seen as an avenue for restoring a semblance of the South's prewar social order. Believing blacks to be inherently inferior, and resentful of their new status as freedmen, the Klansmen surmised that they could frighten the former slaves into resuming their positions as menial laborers and servants for whites. This new purpose—intimidating blacks into continual servitude—hastened the growth of the Klan.

This expansion of the Klan and its development from a fraternity to a terroristic vigilante group is better understood in light of the legislative battle between the North and the South after the Civil War. At war's end, Southern lawmakers had passed measures designed to maintain the social and political dominance of whites in the region. These laws, known as black codes, sharply curtailed the civil rights of the newly freed slaves, making them second-class citizens and essentially returning them to a state of bondage. In response, Northern Republicans passed the Reconstruction Act of 1867, a manuever that temporarily abolished Southern state governments, divided the South into Union-occupied districts, and gave blacks the right to vote and hold political office. With no legal means to maintain the racial caste system that Southerners had long been accustomed to, some former Confederates saw the Klan as the most effective approach to reestablishing white supremacy. As African American studies professor William Banks explains in the documentary *Ku Klux Klan: A Secret History,* "The Reconstruction Klansman saw himself as the *only* vehicle to restore the southern way of life and the social order that had been disrupted by the Civil War."

After the passage of the 1867 Reconstruction Act, the Ku Klux Klan held its first secret convention in Nashville, Tennessee. Former Confederate general Nathan Bedford Forrest was elected as the organization's first Grand Wizard, or national leader. Divulging little of the tactics of intimidation that were to make the group infamous, the Klan's declaration of principles expressed loyalty to the U.S. Constitution and stated that its aim was to "protect the weak, the innocent, and the defenseless from the indignities, wrongs, and outrages of the lawless." And indeed, the Klan's original members were Confederate veterans—many of them law-abiding "southern gentlemen" who believed their intentions were honorable. "These men saw themselves as upholders of the best of their traditions, as protectors of their women, defenders of their homes," writes journalist David Lowe in *Ku Klux Klan: The Invisible Empire.* "They wore white robes, the emblem of purity, and adopted the cross as their symbol."

Despite its organizers' purportedly noble intentions, the Klan became increasingly violent toward the end of the 1860s. In many locales, former members of the prewar vigilante groups that had fought abolitionism joined the Klan and took to whipping, mutilating, or killing their victims when night rides and threats failed to intimidate. Klansmen burned down nearly every black school and church in several Deep South towns. Although the numbers of casualties are unknown, historians estimate that hundreds of African Americans were killed and thousands were injured. Blacks were most often the targets of Klan intimidation, but white schoolteachers from the North, Quakers, Union soldiers, and Republican officials also faced Klan violence.

By 1868 the Klan boasted five hundred thousand members and had become so brutal and uncontrollable that Grand Wizard Forrest, who had denounced terrorism early on, officially disbanded the organization. His order went unheeded. Many local units continued to operate through the early 1870s; there were also groups of men who had never formally joined the Klan but who adopted the Klan's style and tactics as a means to subjugate African Americans. Hundreds of Klansmen and members of similar groups were arrested after Congress passed the Ku Klux Klan Act, which made it a felony "for two or more persons to conspire or go in disguise with the intent to deprive an individual of any civil right or privilege." Although few of these arrests resulted in court trials, Klan activity gradually died out during the late 1870s. With the official end of Reconstruction in 1876, the South was able to reestablish a system of legalized racial segregation. This offered whites of that decade enough reassurance about their dominant social and political status that vigilantism came to be seen as unnecessary.

THE INVISIBLE EMPIRE

In 1915 D.W. Griffith's epic film *The Birth of a Nation* was released. Based on Thomas Dixon's 1905 novel *The Clansman*, Griffith's movie glorified the post–Civil War Klan as a savior of the South from the chaos created by federal Reconstruction policies, Northern carpetbaggers, and blacks who held political office. Klansmen were depicted as chivalrous heroes and protectors of white women while African American men were portrayed as lust-crazed, uncontrollable, and violent. Though it was controversial at the time, the film was enormously successful and provoked popular interest in a Ku Klux Klan revival.

The Birth of a Nation was first shown to Southern audiences just a few days after former Methodist preacher William Joseph Simmons announced the rebirth of the Klan. On Thanksgiving evening in 1915, Simmons led fifteen men to the top of Stone Mountain in a rural area near Atlanta, Georgia, for the first initiation ceremony of the reincarnated order. Renamed Invisible Empire, Knights of the Ku Klux Klan, its membership was open—for an initiation fee of $16.50—to American-born white Protestant males over the age of sixteen. Many historians maintain that Simmons was more interested in reviving the Klan as a fraternal order—similar to the Masons or the Elks—and not as a vigilante group or political organization. According to several analysts, Simmons was also apparently enticed by the potential fortune to be made as the Klan's leader.

The new Klan grew slowly at first, gaining less than two thousand members by 1917. In 1920 Simmons was approached by professional publicists who suggested a recruitment strategy that they believed would increase the Klan's membership—and Simmons's coffers. Focusing on the widespread concerns about public morality and patriotism in the wake of World War I, the new strategy depicted the Klan as a promoter of good, clean living and 100 percent Americanism. The Klan was to tout itself as a law-abiding Christian organization devoted to the United States and to the maintenance of white sovereignty.

The new recruitment strategy worked. In less than a year and a half, the Klan gained over one hundred thousand members. As defenders of Protestant Anglo-Saxon Americanism, Klan organizers now surmised that the enemies of the United States included not just blacks striving for equal rights but also "alien influences" such as Jews, Catholics, and immigrants. Rank-and-file members of the Klan soon began to threaten and terrorize racial and religious minorities. Urban Catholics, Jews, and immigrants were subject to economic boycotts and vandalism; rural blacks faced beatings and cross burnings.

In 1921 the *New York World* and several other newspapers ran a series of articles exposing some of the Klan's atrocities and its leaders' financial mismanagement. A congressional investigation ensued, but it was quickly abandoned because Simmons—described by some observers as having a golden tongue—convincingly denied all accusations against the Klan. Ironically, the negative press coverage and congressional scrutiny seemed to attract even more Klan recruits. By 1922 the order had 3 million members and had expanded into the North and across the country, making it the largest and most influential social organization of the early twentieth century.

The vast majority of Klan members—which included five hundred thousand women at the height of the order's popularity—did not participate in terrorism and vigilantism. Increasingly, however, combative groups of Klansmen engaged in brutal episodes of racial and religious violence. Although blacks were most often the victims of Klan-instigated beatings, floggings, and murders, whites accused of immoral behavior, bootlegging, union organizing, or pro-minority campaigning also faced Klan intimidation. In spite of this burgeoning terror, the revived Klan managed to flourish for a few years because it had tapped into the fear of change and the distrust of "outsiders" that millions of Americans shared at the beginning of the twentieth century. The wild abandonment of the Roaring Twenties, the influx of immigrants into urban areas, the migration of blacks from the South into Northern cities, and the rise of communism made many concerned Americans receptive to organizations claiming to endorse morality and patriotism. As activist Julian Bond explains in the documentary *Ku Klux Klan: A Secret History,* the revived Klan "enjoyed the sympathy of non-members who may not have always condoned the most horrific and brutal acts, but who thought the Klan served a role in helping to tamp down 'dissident' elements in society."

Through the mid-1920s, the Klan's popular appeal made it politically influential. The organization was responsible for the election of sixteen senators—five of whom were Klan members—as well as dozens of sheriffs, mayors, and governors. By 1925, however, inept management and disturbing scandals involving Klan leaders led to a sharp decline in Klan membership. One widely publicized scandal involving D.C. Stephenson, the Grand Dragon (state-level leader) of Indiana, badly damaged the Klan's reputation. Stephenson beat, raped, and mutilated Marge Oberholtzer, a young white woman who later signed a deathbed statement describing the details of the assault. A jury found Stephenson guilty of second-degree murder and sentenced him to life in prison. Abandoned by his former associates, Stephenson decided to release evidence about bribery and other political misdeeds involving Klan leaders. Klan membership then fell from its all-time high of 4 million in 1925 to 50,000 by 1929.

From the 1930s through World War II, the revived Klan remained active only on a small scale in the South, where it continued to terrorize union organizers and black voters. In 1944 the organization formally disbanded when it was unable to pay back taxes owed to the federal government.

AMERICAN ANTI-SEMITISM DURING THE 1920S AND 1930S

The revived Ku Klux Klan was not the only organization during the 1920s that grew as a result of American anxiety surrounding the country's changing economic and social climate. From the end of World War I to the beginning of World War II, hundreds of small far-right extremist groups arose to confront what they believed was a worldwide conspiracy among Jews to take control of every nation. Although not typically defined as racial separatists, these groups greatly influenced the ideologies of many latter twentieth-century white separatists.

The notion that Jews are plotting to take over the world has its origins in the *Protocols of the Elders of Zion*, a nineteenth-century fictional document that many people came to accept as fact. The *Protocols* were alleged to be lectures written by members of a secret Jewish government offering directions on how Jews could rise to power by pitting gentiles against each other. In the United States of the 1920s, automobile magnate Henry Ford was the main publicist of this conspiracy theory about Jewish world domination. Beginning in 1920, Ford's weekly Michigan newspaper, the *Dearborn Independent*, ran a series of articles about "the International Jew" that were later compiled into a book. Jews were blamed for a myriad of social and political ills, as the following excerpt reveals:

> Is it surprising that whichever way you turn to trace the harmful streams of influence that flow through society, you come upon a group of Jews? In baseball corruption—a group of Jews. In exploitative finance—a group of Jews. In theatrical degeneracy—a group of Jews. In liquor propaganda—a group of Jews. In control of national war policies—a group of Jews. In control of the Press through business and financial pressure—a group of Jews. War profiteers, 80 per cent of them—Jews. Organizers of active opposition to Christian laws and customs—Jews.

In 1927, after *The International Jew* incited public protest and was strongly denounced by President Woodrow Wilson, Ford retracted the book's accusations and closed down the *Dearborn Independent*. Yet *The International Jew* remained in circulation. As *Village Voice* reporter James Ridgeway notes in *Blood in the Face*, even during the 1980s the book "could still be found on sale, along with the *Protocols*, at right-wing gatherings in the Midwest."

Among those influenced by the belief in a worldwide Jewish conspiracy were several men who rallied thousands of followers to radical right-wing causes. William Dudley Pelley, who maintained that demons occupied Jewish bodies and that Jewish bankers had masterminded the Great Depression, founded the Silver Shirts in 1933. Modeled after Adolf Hitler's Brown Shirts, the Silver Shirts endorsed fascism, collaborated with the pro-Nazi German-American Bund, and trained for armed insurrection. Another paramilitary organization, the Christian Front, was founded by Father Charles Coughlin, a charismatic radio-show host and Catholic priest whose sermons were broadcast from a working-class neighborhood north of Detroit, Michigan. Coughlin had actually begun his radio career by airing catechism classes and anti-Klan speeches during the mid-1920s, but by the 1930s his lectures focused on the "Jewish money-changers," who he claimed had manipulated the economy, and the dangers of Jewish-backed communism.

In 1938 Coughlin encouraged his listeners to organize a Christian Front that would battle the so-called red front of communism. Coughlinite platoons began assembling secretly for military-style training in major eastern and midwestern cities. Young Christian Front recruits physically assaulted Jews in the streets and vandalized Jewish-owned businesses. By the early 1940s, however, both Pelley and Coughlin—and the movements they founded—were silenced under the influence of Franklin Roosevelt's administration, which was attempting to quell right-wing dissidence. Pelley was accused of sedition and was sentenced to fifteen years in prison, and Coughlin was ordered by the archbishop of Detroit to end his radio broadcasts after several Christian Front followers were arrested for plotting to overthrow the government. Some historical analysts contend that the muzzling of Pelley and Coughlin actually advanced the causes they espoused, as both men came to be perceived as political martyrs among white resistance groups of the latter twentieth century.

Another instrumental figure of the 1930s' radical right was Gerald L.K. Smith, founder of the Christian Nationalist Crusade, an ultra-conservative political party. Smith joined Pelley's Silver Shirts in 1933; in 1934 he worked as an organizer in populist politican Huey Long's campaign to redistribute wealth in America. After Long's assassination in 1935, Smith briefly collaborated with Charles Coughlin in an unsuccessful attempt to build a third major political party. An engaging and provocative orator, Smith drew large crowds; through much of the rest of the century he ran for various political offices and rallied support for candidates who opposed civil rights, racial integration, and liberalism. Smith also associated with several preachers who were to form Christian Identity, a religious group based on the belief that the white race was specially chosen as God's people.

WESLEY SWIFT AND CHRISTIAN IDENTITY

Wesley Swift, a Protestant minister and an aide to Gerald Smith, founded the Church of Jesus Christ Christian in Lancaster, California, at the end of World War II. Swift championed an American variation of British-Israelism, a nineteenth-century theological doctrine claiming that the Anglo-Saxon-Celtic people are the true descendants of the biblical lost tribes of Israel. In the United States, under the influence of clergymen who believed that Jews were plotting to take over the world, British-Israelism evolved into Christian Identity. The basic tenets of Christian Identity include the notion that nonwhites are soulless beings created before Adam and that Jews are the offspring that resulted from Eve's sexual relationship with Satan—who had seduced her in the guise of a nonwhite being. According to Christian Identity, white "Aryans" are the true descendants of Adam and Eve and the Israelites of the Bible, and miscegenation is the "original sin" that brought evil into the world. Christian Identity adherents also contend that the world is on the verge of a final battle between good and evil, with Aryans battling Jews in order to bring about Christ's kingdom on Earth. Swift died in 1970, but some of his congregants and sympathizers became leaders in modern-day white separatist groups such the White Aryan Resistance, Aryan Nations, and the Order.

WHITE SEPARATISM DURING THE CIVIL RIGHTS ERA

In May 1954 the U.S. Supreme Court declared school segregation unconstitutional, arguing that racially separate education was inherently unequal and kept deeply entrenched patterns of discrimination intact. Integrating public schools, supporters surmised, would be an important step toward dismantling racial discrimination and promoting equal opportunity for black Americans.

This 1954 Supreme Court decision sparked America's civil rights movement—an upsurge of grassroots political activity aimed at overturning segregation laws in the South and obtaining civil liberties for African Americans in all states. From the mid-1950s through the end of the 1960s, civil rights activists organized boycotts, protests, and demonstrations in support of desegregation, and a series of new federal laws outlawed racial discrimination in housing, employment, and public accommodations.

For civil rights supporters, the condemnation of school segregation may have seemed like a harbinger of freedom. But for Southern white segregationists, the day of the 1954 Supreme Court ruling came to be known as Black Monday. Alabama state senator Walter C. Givhan railed against the campaign to end school segregation, arguing that its true purpose was "to open the bedroom doors of our white women to Negro men." The South witnessed an increase of beatings, burnings, and lynchings of blacks by mobs of whites. New white separatist organizations formed, and a few defunct groups reemerged.

One of the new separatist groups, the Citizens' Council,

held its first meeting in Mississippi just two months after the May 1954 Supreme Court decision. Distinguishing itself from the more militant Klan, the Citizen's Council was composed of middle-class, educated, law-abiding professionals who sought to control blacks more through economic intimidation than by violence. One council leader, for example, proclaimed that the group's purpose was "to make it difficult, if not impossible, for any Negro who advocates desegregation to find and hold a job, get credit, or renew a mortgage." Citizens' Councils—which came to be known as White Citizens' Councils—spread throughout the South during the 1950s and 1960s and influenced segregationist thought through their newspaper, the *Councilor*.

One organization whose ideas on race were largely influenced by the writings of the Citizens' Council was the John Birch Society. Founded in 1958 by Massachusetts candy maker Robert Welch, the John Birch Society began as a secret group that intended to save America from the "international communist plot." The John Birch Society opposed all federal activities that it believed were attempts at collectivism and governmental control of society, including the graduated income tax, social security, water fluoridation, housing aid, and "forced integration." By the 1960s society members were declaring that the civil rights movement was "Communist-controlled" and served only "Communist purposes." As part of its anti–civil rights drive, the organization set up front groups known as Truth About Civil Turmoil (TACT). Ironically, TACT committees posed as black support groups and included right-wing blacks as members. Birch members and supporters longed for a return to the Jim Crow South of the earlier twentieth century, when there was, in Welch's words, "a huge reservoir of good will between the races," and "a very, very tiny amount of injustice."

Both the Citizens' Council and the John Birch Society believed that racial segregation was a valuable American tradition and one of the hallmarks of a moral society. This view was supported by many ordinary Americans, particularly

Southerners, during the middle of the twentieth century. A large percentage of whites endorsed the laws that had required the separation of the races in almost all aspects of life. Intended to ensure that African Americans maintained a menial status in the absence of slavery, legalized segregation had also worked to "protect" whites from the distasteful attributes they had come to associate with blacks: violence, uncleanliness, and immorality. The stereotype of blacks as lazy, intellectually inferior, and savage—rooted in a worldview that developed early in America's history—lingered long after the end of slavery. These long-held assumptions continued to influence American attitudes, and people often saw segregation as the normal way of life, the proper social standard. Many analysts maintain that the beliefs of the Citizens' Councils and the Birchers, therefore, were simply a more extreme version of commonly held American views on race.

THE MINUTEMEN AND THE AMERICAN NAZI PARTY

Although the White Citizens' Councils and the John Birch Society did not advocate violence or the overthrow of the U.S. government, other groups touting anticommunism and segregation promoted more radical means of maintaining racial separation. In 1960 former John Birch Society member and chemical company owner Robert DePugh started the Minutemen, "a national organization of patriotic Americans who are preparing themselves as a last line of defense against communism." The strategy of the Minutemen was to build a guerrilla army trained in sophisticated weaponry and biological and chemical warfare. DePugh compiled a list of fifteen hundred "traitors"—members of what he believed was a secret Communist government—and marked them for assassination in the event of a government coup. The Minutemen launched several failed offensives, including an attempted assassination of Arkansas senator William Fulbright and an unsuccessful plan to attack the United Nations by poisoning its ventilation system.

The Minutemen forged alliances with several like-minded

groups during the 1960s. One such group was Wesley Swift's Church of Jesus Christ Christian, the Christian Identity organization that later evolved into the Aryan Nations. DePugh's organization also sheltered and spawned a number of paramilitary orders, including the Sons of Liberty and the Soldiers of the Cross, whose adherents often had dual memberships in the Ku Klux Klan or the American Nazi Party.

The American Nazi Party was started by George Lincoln Rockwell, an advertising illustrator who had served as a U.S. Navy pilot during World War II and the Korean War. Influenced by the thinking of charismatic right-wing politician Gerald L.K. Smith, Rockwell worked for the United White Party and the National Committee to Free America from Jewish Domination before founding the American Nazi Party in 1958. The goal of Rockwell and his followers was to "exterminate Jewish traitors," to "send all blacks back to Africa," and "to prevent further mongrelization" of the white race. Known for being bold and outrageous, Rockwell stirred controversy by giving provocative speeches on college campuses and by picketing both black activists and white conservatives. In 1967 he was assassinated by one of his own disgruntled former lieutenants. Although the American Nazi Party probably had only two thousand members at its peak, many modern-day white separatists consider the group an important part of their history.

THE KU KLUX KLAN DURING THE 1960S

In 1946 Atlanta physician Samuel Green established the Association of Georgia Klans. This organization was the first in a series of small, independent Klan groups that sprang up after World War II. Encountering strong opposition from some state legislatures, these new Klans were unable to amass as large a following as the Klan of the 1920s. Several states, including California and New York, banned the organization. In 1947 U.S. attorney general Tom Clark placed the Klan on his so-called subversives list. One year after its formation, the Association of Georgia Klans had its charter revoked by the state of Georgia.

As was the case with several other separatist groups, however, Klan membership increased after the 1954 Supreme Court decision outlawing school segregation. In 1961 Freedom Riders—students and civil rights workers chartering Greyhound buses to challenge segregation in public accommodations—descended upon the South. In Birmingham and Montgomery, Alabama, Klan-led mobs attacked newly arrived Freedom Riders with clubs and pipes, prompting Attorney General Robert Kennedy to send five hundred marshals to the state. Confronted with this sudden upsurge in civil rights activism, several Klan groups held a conference in Georgia and created a new organization: The United Klans of America (UKA), headed by Robert Shelton. The UKA was to be the largest of the dozens of Klan groups that formed during the latter half of the twentieth century.

Klan members and Klan sympathizers were implicated in several high-profile bombings and murders during the civil rights era. In September 1963 the Sixteenth Street Baptist Church in Birmingham, Alabama, was bombed, killing four black teenage girls. The Federal Bureau of Investigation (FBI) named four suspects in the bombing—two with Klan affiliations—but at the time none of them were charged with a crime. (In 1971 Alabama attorney general Bill Baxley reopened the case, resulting in a 1977 murder conviction for Klan member Robert Chambliss.) In June 1964 civil rights workers James Chaney, Andrew Goodman, and Michael Schwerner were killed near Philadelphia, Mississippi. J. Edgar Hoover, chief of the FBI, dispatched 153 FBI agents and 400 navy troops to investigate the crime, arousing press coverage and national indignation over the killings. Eventually, seven men—including the head of the White Knights of the Ku Klux Klan and a deputy sheriff—were convicted. In March 1965 white civil rights worker Viola Liuzzo was shot and killed in Loundes County, Alabama, as she drove a black youth in her car. Three Klansmen were convicted on federal civil rights charges and were sentenced to ten years in prison. Many of the thousands of incidents of racial violence between 1955 and 1965—including 225 bombings and more than 40 murders of civil rights activists—were attributed to Klansmen or Klan sympathizers. In several locales, support for Klan activity among law enforcement and the citizenry enabled perpetrators to avoid prosecution and conviction.

The civil rights movement's desegregation efforts had initially been met with massive popular resistance in the South. Even in the urban North, civil rights activists had been scorned as outside agitators invading the South to force integration on the population. But the deaths of four young girls at a church and the high-profile killings of black and white civil rights workers shocked the nation and ultimately galvanized support for the goals of the civil rights movement. Unwittingly, the Klan's tactics of intimidation actually benefited the cause its members sought to destroy. As journalist James Ridgeway notes, "The Klan's violence and seeming invulnerability to prosecution eventually helped the civil rights movement. Just as Congress had passed the Civil Rights Act shortly after the killings of Schwerner, Chaney, and Goodman, the Voting Rights Act was enacted into law in the aftermath of the Liuzzo murder."

Klan membership dwindled from approximately forty thousand in 1961 to a low of fifteen hundred in 1973. Through the mid-1970s, the FBI's infiltration of Klan groups, as well as the increasing popular acceptance of the civil rights cause, made it more difficult for the organization to recruit new members.

WHITE SEPARATISM DURING THE LATE TWENTIETH CENTURY

During the late twentieth century the United States witnessed an apparent increase in the number of groups advocating the separation of the races and the establishment of white rule, or a white homeland. These groups included various new Klan chapters, spinoffs and outgrowths of the American Nazi Party, Christian Identity sects and their affiliates, and loosely organized gangs of white separatist skinheads. Although relations among these groups were often characterized by rivalry and infighting, occasional alliances among Klansmen, neo-Nazis, and skinheads spawned the development of new organizations that eventually drew younger middle-class recruits. One major event that reveals connections between different white separatist groups was the November 3, 1979, incident in Greensboro, North Carolina. At an anti-Klan rally sponsored by the Communist Workers Party, five Communist activists were killed during a shootout between demonstrators and a group of both neo-Nazis and Klansmen.

After the Greensboro incident, several civil rights groups and antiracist political organizations stepped up their efforts to organize community opposition to Klan and neo-Nazi groups. One organization, the Southern Poverty Law Center (SPLC), would prove to be a formidable challenge to the more militant white separatist groups. Founded in 1971 by Democratic political consultant Morris Dees, Montgomery attorney Joe Levin, and civil rights leader Julian Bond, the center dedicated itself to advancing the legal rights of minorities and the poor through education and litigation. In the last two decades of the twentieth century the center's legal team won several lawsuits on behalf of individuals who had been attacked by members of white separatist organizations. In one of its first major victories the SPLC won a judgment against six Klansmen for the 1981 lynching of a black teenager. The United Klans of America was then forced to sell its headquarters and give the money to the mother of the deceased.

DAVID DUKE AND TOM METZGER

Associations between several dedicated separatists during the 1970s laid the groundwork for white separatist group operations during the last two decades of the twentieth century. In 1975 budding politician David Duke took over the leadership of the Knights of the Ku Klux Klan in Louisiana. Young, articulate, and handsome, Duke attempted to give the Klan mainstream appeal by recruiting on college campuses, accepting women as equal members, and inviting Catholics to join. He organized various local Klan units in several states, but he resigned from his post in 1980 to found a new organization that he felt would attract more of the middle class: the National Association for the Advancement of White People (NAAWP). The NAAWP defined itself as a civil rights organization that "believes that White people need to defend and preserve their civil rights, heritage, and basic interests, just as Blacks and other non-Whites do." Duke ran for political office several times, including a 1988 and 1992 run for president; in 1989 he won a seat in the Louisiana state house of representatives. Duke's 1988 campaign manager, Ralph Forbes, was a former member of Rockwell's American Nazi Party.

Another former American Nazi, James K. Warner, paved the way for a brief alliance between Duke and another influential white separatist, former John Birch Society member Tom Metzger. In 1971 Warner had opened a Christian Identity church in Los Angeles; four years later Metzger was ordained there as a Christian Identity minister. In 1975 Warner became director of information for David Duke's Klan, and he soon introduced Metzger to Duke. Metzger ran the California branch of Duke's Klan, but he dropped his Christian Identity ministry and his association with Duke to establish his own special "klavern" (Klan meeting place) in 1981. After several runs for political office, Metzger broke off with the Klan completely and founded the intentionally militant-sounding White American Resistance (WAR) in 1983. Metzger describes WAR as "a deliberate move to scare off the weak-kneed people from my group." Furthermore, he explains, "I shifted my stance and became more anti-system than ever. I condemned the federal government, the idle rich, the one-party political system, the 'minorities,' and the white public at large, for being worthless hypocrites." By 1984 Metzger had changed the name of WAR to White Aryan Resistance. Along with his son, John, he began to seek out recruits among the growing number of American skinheads.

SKINHEADS IN THE UNITED STATES

The origins of skinheads in the United States can be traced back to England of the 1960s, when a youthful delinquent subculture arose to protest the social and economic problems facing British working-class communities. By the late 1960s cropped hair, big boots, and cuffed jeans identified one as a skinhead who was rejecting the "elitist" values of the long-haired, middle-class hippies. Some skinheads, perceiving immigrants as threats to British workers, engaged in racial attacks—particularly against Pakistani, Caribbean, and African immigrants. (Other groups of skinheads, however, vigorously opposed racism and forged alliances with minorities.) During the 1980s the anti-immigrant segment of skinhead culture came under the influence of musician and publicist Ian Stuart, a member of a neo-fascist organization known as the British National Front. Stuart's band, Skrewdriver, popularized a "white power" variant of punk rock and traditional pub "Oi" music. Stuart's music, videos, and publications appealed to a sector of disaffected, unemployed white youth across Europe, spawning and influencing skinhead movements in France, Germany, Hungary, Poland, and Russia.

During the 1980s white youth gangs patterning themselves after the European skinheads emerged in Chicago, San Francisco, Cincinnati, Milwaukee, and Portland. A flier printed by Cincinnati's White American Skinheads describes the members of its group as "working-class Aryan youth" who are "proud to be White, Gentile, and American. We would prefer to smash the present anti-White, Zionist (Jew) puppet run government with a healthy, new, White man's order!" Skinheads gained notoriety as an increasing number of them painted racist graffiti, defaced synagogues, and engaged in assaults against Jews and minorities.

Several white separatist organizations came to see skinheads as the foot soldiers of the movement and began recruiting them. Metzger, for example, familiarized himself with the British skinhead scene and began publishing *WAR*, a youth-oriented magazine with articles and comics lauding racial violence, addresses of avowed skinheads, and order forms for purchasing white power music, videos, clothing, and posters. According to researcher Mark S. Hamm, author of *American*

Skinheads, Metzger's aim was to "inject some ideology into the skinheads," and to strengthen "the emerging global struggle of whites against Jews and mongrels." Metzger also orchestrated an assertive campaign involving computer links, phone hot lines, and media appearances that drew national attention during the late 1980s. American skinheads were seen on several popular talk shows, including one appearance that escalated into a televised brawl during which host Geraldo Rivera's nose was broken.

In November 1988—one night after the fight on *Geraldo*—Ethiopian immigrant Mulugeta Seraw was killed by three white skinheads in Portland, Oregon. Two years later, the SPLC won a $12.5-million civil suit against the Metzger family for the death of Seraw. Metzger and his son, John, were declared liable for Seraw's murder because they had originally recruited the skinheads and had encouraged them to participate in violent behavior against nonwhites.

CHRISTIAN IDENTITY AND NEO-NAZIS

Skinheads have also been recruited by several groups that emerged as outgrowths of Wesley Swift's Church of Jesus Christ Christian. After Swift's death in 1970, Richard Butler, a manufacturing engineer for Lockheed Aircraft, took charge of the church. Butler moved to northern Idaho in 1973 and established a Christian Identity organization near Hayden Lake. This group became known as Aryan Nations–Church of Jesus Christ Christian, commonly referred to as Aryan Nations (AN). Butler set up a twenty-acre compound, complete with a church-school and a paramilitary training facility, which became a gathering place for militant white separatists during the 1980s and 1990s.

Starting in 1982, AN held annual Congresses in which skinheads, Klansmen, and neo-Nazis would congregate to hear speeches by group representatives and to learn about white separatist politics and culture. Among the conference attractions was a book entitled *The Turner Diaries* by Andrew Mac-Donald, a pseudonym for William Pierce. Pierce, a former physics professor, had been a John Birch Society member and a publicist for Rockwell's American Nazi Party before forming a group called the National Alliance during the late 1960s. Claiming that the white race is inherently superior to all other races and that whites should take action to preserve their gene pool, the National Alliance seeks recruits through its publications and its radio program, *American Dissident Voices*.

Pierce's *Turner Diaries*, first printed in 1978, became infamous for the role some observers believe it played in fomenting late twentieth-century domestic terrorism. The novel details the actions of Earl Turner, a white youth who becomes a member of an underground group called the Order. Turner and his comrades use terrorism to spearhead a revolution meant to liberate Aryans from the tyranny of government-enforced multiculturalism. At the end of the book, the United States is purged of non-Aryans and disloyal whites.

In September 1983 former John Birch Society member Robert Mathews created an organization called the Order, also known as the Silent Brotherhood. Members—generally supporters of National Alliance and Aryan Nations—saw themselves as revolutionaries fighting against a society trying to destroy the white race. To raise money for the white militant cause, the Order robbed millions of dollars from banks, malls, and armored cars; the group also drew up a hit list of enemies, including Morris Dees of the SPLC, television producer Norman Lear, and controversial radio talk-show host Alan Berg. Order members actually phoned in to Berg's talk show and argued with him on the air. In June 1984 several Order members followed Berg home from work and machine-gunned him to death. By December of that year, the FBI had connected a weapon used in one of the Order's robberies to Mathews. Mathews was then traced to an island off of Washington State, where he was shot and killed after a thirty-six-hour standoff. Ultimately, twenty-four Order members were arrested on robbery and murder charges, and ten were convicted and sentenced to lengthy prison terms.

On April 19, 1995, a bomb blast destroyed the Alfred P.

Murrah Federal Building in Oklahoma City, killing 168 people. Many analysts initially presumed that such a large act of terrorism must have been committed by foreigners with hostility toward the United States. Americans were therefore shocked to learn that the two main suspects in the bombing, Timothy McVeigh and Terry Nichols, were native-born Americans with ties to antigovernment militias. Although McVeigh was not known to be a member of a white separatist group, he had sold copies of *The Turner Diaries* at gun shows and survivalist conventions. The details of the Oklahoma City blast eerily echoed the fictional bombing of the FBI head-quarters depicted in *The Turner Diaries*. Both suspects were con-victed; Nichols received a federal life sentence while McVeigh was sentenced to death and was executed in June 2001.

The Oklahoma City bombing, along with the seeming in-crease in bias-motivated crimes during the 1980s and 1990s, stepped up legislative efforts to pass a law that would allow the federal government to prosecute any violent crime inspired by bigotry. Although some communities have laws that impose additional prison time or higher fines for hate crimes, federal administration of such crimes is limited, and punishments vary from state to state. Supporters of a federal hate crimes law maintain that since bias-motivated offenses can fragment com-munities and damage the nation as a whole, federal involve-ment is warranted. Critics, however, argue that such a measure would violate the First Amendment by allowing the govern-ment to punish bigoted thoughts and attitudes. Authorities should punish criminal activity itself, these critics insist—not the bias that might motivate such activity.

As of 2001 the proposed Federal Hate Crimes Prevention Act had not passed. The SPLC's legal team, however, has con-tinued to win civil lawsuits on behalf of individuals who have been attacked by members of militant white separatist groups. In September 2000 a jury awarded Victoria and Jason Keenan $6.3 million in their suit against Richard Butler and the Aryan Nations. Two years earlier the Native American mother and son had been chased and shot at by Aryan Nations security guards near the group's Idaho compound. As a result of the lawsuit, Butler was required to hand over the twenty-acre compound to the Keenans. The Keenans decided to sell the land to a philanthropist, who plans to create a center for tolerance on the property.

WHY DO PEOPLE JOIN WHITE SEPARATIST GROUPS?

What might account for the proliferation of white separatist groups after the 1980s? Many analysts point to the nation's fluctuating economy, which has led to corporate downsizing and job loss among white men. Some whites see themselves as losing their jobs to minority group members, particularly immigrants—making them more vulnerable to anxieties about growing populations of nonwhites and the possibility that whites will soon become a minority group. Jared Taylor, editor of the anti-integrationist journal *American Renaissance*, expressed some of these anxieties in a 1996 speech:

> I am quite certain that my ancestors didn't fight for independence from Britain in order for our generation to turn the country over to Mexicans and Haitians. The Founders didn't frame the Constitution to celebrate diversity. . . . And yet, the rightful heirs to what could have been a shining beacon of Western Civilization are giving up their country without a struggle. What we are witnessing is one of the great tragedies in human history. Powerful forces are in motion that, if left unchecked, will slowly push aside European man and European civilization and then dance a victory jig on their collective grave. If we do nothing, the nation we leave to our children will be a desolated, third-world failure, in which whites will be a despised minority.

But many observers find it difficult to understand the interest in white separatist groups among young people raised in tolerant homes. Sharon and Thomas Leydon of Fontana, California, who claim that they had raised their son, Thomas Jr., to abhor racism, were horrified when he became a neo-

Nazi skinhead. Leydon, who eventually renounced his neo-Nazi beliefs, maintains that his transformation began with the anger and loneliness surrounding his parents' divorce when he was fifteen. "I needed to lash out," states Leydon. "They [skinhead recruiters] look for young, angry kids who need a family. . . . I thought I was being patriotic." Another former skinhead, Mark Flanigan, also contends that the economic hardships and alienation he experienced while he was growing up made him a good candidate for membership in a neo-Nazi group. Such groups tend to provide easy answers to complex problems, Flanigan maintains, which make them attractive to unhappy people.

Leydon was prompted to leave the separatist movement when he became concerned about the future of his young son. As he explains in an interview with an SPLC journalist:

> We were watching a Caribbean-style show. My three-year-old walked over to the TV, turned it off and said, "Daddy, we don't watch shows with niggers." My first impression was, "Wow, this kid's pretty cool." Then I started seeing something different. I started seeing my son act like someone ten times tougher than I was, ten times more loyal, and I thought he'd end up actually doing something and going to prison. Or he was going to get hurt or killed.
>
> I started looking at the hypocrisy. A white guy, even if he does crystal meth and sells crack to kids, if he's a Nazi he's okay. And yet this black gentleman here, who's got a Ph.D and is helping out white kids, he's still a "scummy nigger."
>
> In 1996, when I was at the Aryan Nations Congress, I started listening to everybody and felt like, "God, this is pathetic." I asked the guy sitting next to me, "If we wake up tomorrow and the race war is over and we've won, what are we going to do next?" And he said, "Oh, come on, T.J., you know we're going to start with hair color next, dude."
>
> I laughed at it, but when I drove home, 800 miles, that question and answer kept popping into my head. I thought that

kid was so right. Next it'll be you have black hair so you can't be white . . . or you wear glasses so you have a genetic defect.

A little over two years after my son said the thing about "niggers" on TV, I left the racist movement.

The white separatist movement faces an uncertain future. Some militant groups, such as the Order, have disappeared as their leaders faced criminal convictions and prison sentences. Other groups, such as White Aryan Resistance and Aryan Nations, have been weakened, at least temporarily, by liability lawsuits. The dwindling membership of the Ku Klux Klan was partly a result of FBI infiltration of the organization. Some critics caution, however, that well-meaning attempts to curtail the activities of white separatist groups could backfire if such efforts become overly repressive. As researchers Dobratz and Shanks-Meile point out, "Repression could provide a means to unify the movement and attract additional support for it." The future of the white separatist movement, they note, likely depends on a number of historical factors—"some that the movement can help shape and some that the movement may well not be able to control."

CHAPTER 1

THE ORIGINAL KU KLUX KLAN

AMERICAN
SOCIAL
MOVEMENTS

A Historical Overview of the First Ku Klux Klan

PAUL J. GILLETTE AND EUGENE TILLINGER

In the following selection, journalists Paul J. Gillette and Eugene Tillinger point out that secret terroristic societies existed prior to the birth of the Ku Klux Klan. These groups intimidated and assaulted people who opposed slavery and Southern states' rights. Although the Klan itself began in the spirit of mischief, its secret nighttime intimidation campaigns against the occupying Northern army began to attract men who had belonged to the pre–Civil War terroristic societies. Soon Klan members were torturing and lynching blacks in retaliation for their alleged crimes against whites. General Nathan Bedford Forrest, the Klan's first national leader, ordered the disbanding of the Klan once he learned of the group's atrocities. Yet Klan violence continued long after Forrest's edict.

The Klan came into its own as a terrorist group in the late 1860s, but organizations of similar purpose and scope existed throughout the South during roughly two decades before the Civil War. As abolitionists clamored for the freedom of Negro slaves, secret groups prowled the countryside beating, castrating and sometimes even murdering persons suspected of harboring antislavery views.

The best-known terrorist group during the 1840s and '50s was the Knights of the Golden Circle. An allied organization was the Minute Men. Also prominent on the scene were The Precipitation and the Knights of the Columbian Order. All were pledged to stop at nothing in their war against the "en-

Excerpted from *Inside Ku Klux Klan*, by Paul J. Gillette and Eugene Tillinger (New York: Pyramid Books, 1965).

emies" of "southern rights" (or, as a clever propagandist was later to dub them, *"states' rights"*). All operated as "secret" societies with mysterious passwords, exotic ceremonials and far-flung networks of local sub-units.

Persons caught distributing anti-slavery pamphlets or otherwise overtly aiding the abolitionist cause were invariably visited by one or more of these groups. First offenders were usually let off with a beating or flogging and a warning; second offenders were summarily lynched. As years passed and anti-North sentiments grew stronger, the warnings for first offenders were suspended—and some people were murdered merely because they were *suspected* of opposing secession. In the years immediately prior to 1861, there were on record in Florida, Georgia, Mississippi, Alabama, Louisiana and South Carolina literally hundreds of cases where men were hanged by mobs simply because they had expressed sentiments not hostile to the United (as opposed to the Confederate) States.

After the firing on Fort Sumter, most groups were weakened as their members went into battle with the Confederate Army. By the time Robert E. Lee surrendered at Appomatox, the Knights of the Golden Circle and the Minute Men were out of business completely; the Knights of the Columbian Order and The Precipitation existed only as disgruntled and impotent bands of "old-timers."

THE BIRTH OF THE KLAN

In December 1865, at Pulaski, Tennessee, a group of Confederate Army veterans and non-military students joined together to form the Ku Klux Klan. The organization's aims were more in the spirit of "mischief" than terrorism; by night-riding and similar clandestine activities, it was felt, they could harass and annoy the occupation forces of the Blue Army. The original plan was to operate under the name, Knights of the Circle; but, since it was believed that this might result in the group's being confused with the now-defunct Knights of the Golden Circle, one member suggested the name, Knights of the Kuklos. (*Kuklos* is the Greek word for "circle.") Impressed with the alliterative properties of the letter "K," members later settled upon Kuklos Klan and, finally *Ku Klux Klan.*

Subsequently, an entire line of K-initialed nomenclature was established to designate the various offices, symbols and artifacts of the Klan. The deserted mansion in which members convened was called the *Klavern.* The men assigned to guard it were designated *Klexters* and *Klaragos.* A schedule of *Klectokons,* or dues, was drawn up, and a *Klabee,* or treasurer, was appointed to collect them. *Kleagles,* or organizers, were selected to recruit new members, and *Knight-hawks* were named to initiate them. *Klodes,* or anthems, were composed, and a *Kludd,* or chaplain, was elected to lead their recitation. A *Kladd* or password boss, was put in charge of security matters, and *Klokans,* or investigators, were assigned to assist him. The only officer whose title did not begin with a "K" was the *Exalted Cyclops,* or president. His assistants were a *Klailiff,* or vice-president, and a *Kligrapp,* or secretary. The entire system was called *Klancraft,* and the means of communication, *Klanguage.*

Soon, the old-time terrorists of the Golden Circle, Minute Men, Columbian Order and Precipitation groups began to view the newly organized Klan as the answer to their dreams: Here was a ready-made secret order whose structure lent itself perfectly to the conduct of intimidation campaigns. One by one, the old-timers began to infiltrate; before long, the Klan's membership-seeking Kleagles found themselves swamped with more applications than they could handle. Sub-units, called *dens,* began springing up all over the South—and, in 1867, little more than a year after the first organizational meeting, a *national convention* was held at Nashville to establish a hierarchy of Klan leadership.

THE INVISIBLE EMPIRE

The whole of Klandom, it was decided, would be called *The Invisible Empire.* It would be presided over by a *Grand Wizard of the Empire,* assisted by a cabinet of ten *Genii.* These would include a *Grand Kleagle,* or chief-of-staff; a *Grand Klailiff,* or vice-president; a *Grand Kligrapp,* or secretary, and so on down the line.

The Empire was broken down into *Realms,* each consisting of one state. A *Grand Dragon of the Realm* was put in command, aided by a cabinet of eight *Hydras.* Each realm was subdivided into *Dominions,* presided over by a *Grand Titan of the Dominion* and six *Furies.* Each dominion was subdivided into *Provinces,* with a *Grand Giant* and four *Goblins.* Finally came the *Den,* with its *Grand Cyclops* and two *Knight-Hawks.* Some dens, fearing that the K-initialed offices sounded too ludicrous to entice serious members, were given permission to name their leaders *Grand Magi, Grand Exchequer, Grand Turk, Grand Scribe, Grand Sentinel* and *Grand Ensign* instead.

After this table of organization was drawn up, it came time to elect the Grand Wizard of the Empire. Nominated and elected by acclamation was the popular Confederate cavalryman, General Nathan Bedford Forrest. Other national officers included planters, politicians and businessmen who had been turned out of power by the Loyal Leagues of Reconstruction and the Negro Unions.

KLAN ATROCITIES

With Forrest as a figure-head, the Klan grew in leaps and bounds. By 1868, the membership totalled more than 500,000 and the Klan-perpetrated atrocities, incited by the infiltrating old-timers from the prewar groups, numbered well into the millions. Behind the anonymity of their hoods and robes, Klansmen rode the highways and country lanes, burning houses and farms, whipping and flogging Federal sympathizers and massacring Negroes. If a black man was believed to be guilty of having seduced a white woman, he was castrated, tarred and feathered, then lynched. Likewise, if a white woman was believed to have encouraged the sexual advances of a black man, she was murdered—usually only after she had been shaven bald and made to parade through the streets nude, the words "nigger-lover" painted across (or carved by pen-knife into) her chest and back.

Local law enforcement agencies calmly turned their backs to what was going on. While crimes were being committed, cops conveniently happened to be elsewhere. By the time the deed had been done, evidence was "insufficient to warrant arrest." In effect, Kluxers had legal *carte blanche*—and they exercised it with impunity.

In Doddsville, Miss., an eyewitness to the lynching of Mr. and Mrs. Luther Holbert, gave this account to *The Vicksburg Evening Post:*

> When the two negroes were captured, they were tied to trees, and, while the funeral pyres were being prepared, they were forced to hold out their hands while one finger at a time was chopped off. The fingers were distributed as souvenirs. The ears of the murderers were cut off. Holbert was beaten severely, his skull was fractured and one of his eyes, knocked out with a stick, hung by a shred from the socket.
>
> Some of the mob used a large corkscrew to bore into the flesh of the man and the woman. It was applied to their arms, legs and bodies, then pulled out, the spirals tearing out big pieces of raw, quivering flesh every time it was withdrawn. A young son was made to witness the event.

In Knoxville, Tenn., meanwhile, Ed Johnson, a Negro convicted of rape—by an all-Caucasian jury—was lynched by an hysterical mob after word was received that the United States Supreme Court had granted him an appeal. In Jennings, La., Negro James Comeaux was lynched after he struck a merchant who had swept dirt on his shoes. And in Plaquemine, La., a mob hanged Negro William Carr for allegedly killing a "white" man's cow!

From Centreville, Ala., *The Montgomery Advertiser* reported: "Grant Richardson, a negro, was lynched tonight by a party of angry miners. Some months ago, a white woman named Mrs. Crow gave birth to a child of doubtful color. It was thought by townspeople that this child bore a resemblance to Richardson." And, in Louisville, Ky., according to *The Birmingham News,* "Henry Crosby, a negro of Parksville, was lynched after frightening a farmer's wife. He had entered the house of Mrs. J.C. Carroll and asked whether her husband was at home."

A Patina of Unconcern

The nonchalance with which the newspapers wrote of racial atrocities is especially revealing of the temper of the times. *The Birmingham News,* for example, quite unexcitedly observed that "a negro was strung up and shot to pieces by a mob today when rumor swept through the town (of Pensacola, Fla.) that he had loaned an amulet to a suspected murderer." Apparently the editors considered the man's identity insignificant; they didn't even bother to print his name.

Nor was this patina of unconcern the exclusive property of the South. *The Chicago Defender,* not the slightest bit outraged, reported that "Mrs. Cordella Stevenson, negro, was raped by a mob of white men and lynched after she told local police that she did not know the whereabouts of her son, who is suspected of barn-burning."

A particularly revolting example of mob brutality was the lynching in Rome, Tenn., of Miss Ballie Crutchfield. A mob of several hundred Kluxers stormed her home at midnight, hauled her out of bed and dragged her through the dirt-and-gravel streets leading to Round Lick Creek, on the outskirts of town. There they tied her hands with hemp behind her bloodied, gravel-pitted back; knotted a burlap sack over her head and took turns raping her; then shot her through the head and dumped her lifeless body into the creek.

Their motive? "The mob," reported *The New York Tribune,* "was looking for William Crutchfield, brother of the victim, in connection with the theft of a purse. Unable to find him, they lynched Ballie Crutchfield instead."

And, from Savannah, Ga., this unspeakably atrocious report by *The Chicago Record-Herald:*

A mob lynched the wrong negro at Eastman, it was learned last night. The victim was not Ed Claus, suspected of raping a school teacher, but a different young negro. The real Claus was located near Darien yesterday.

Before the lynching, the victim had protested that he was not Claus, had never met the school teacher and pleaded for time to prove his innocence. It is expected that the real Ed Claus will be lynched shortly.

GENERAL FORREST'S DISCLAIMER

General Forrest, himself, disclaimed any knowledge of these happenings—at least, insofar as the Klan was involved. Any person could don a robe and hood and commit a crime, he pointed out; until there was concrete evidence of Klan involvement, the organization must be presumed innocent. In a speech at Washington in 1868, he declared that the K.K.K. was a "protective, political, military organization" that condoned no wrongdoing and sternly disapproved of anyone taking the law into his own hands. If it could be proved that a Klansman had been involved in any crime, he promised, the Klan would immediately suspend him—and offer law enforcement agencies every assistance in bringing him to justice.

In retrospect, it appears that Forrest was sincere (if blind) in his beliefs. A year after his Washington speech, he conferred with Federal agents who proved conclusively that his Klansmen were responsible for the majority of "unsolved" atrocities in a tri-state area. Promptly, the general issued an order disbanding the Klan. Then, he made a public statement personally disassociating himself from all Klansmen and promising to assist authorities in breaking up those recalcitrant groups and sub-groups that ignored the formal disband order.

Unfortunately, Forrest's assistance proved to be useless. The Klan created by him and his cohorts had become a Frankensteinian force they could neither control nor subdue. Despite the efforts of responsible Southern leaders and Federal officials, the night rides continued and the atrocities mounted.

A FEARFUL CONSPIRACY

On February 19, 1872, the Second Session of the 42nd Congress took under consideration the *Report of the Joint Select Committee of the House of Representatives on the Condition of Affairs in the Late Insurrectionary States*. The report noted literally thousands of instances of Klan-inspired violence, destruction and murder. In Mississippi, schoolhouses had been destroyed and teachers driven away. In Georgia and South Carolina, the rate of unsolved murders was more than one per month. From Texas, General William Reynolds, commander of the Federal forces, reported: "Murders of Negroes are so common as to render it impossible to keep an accurate account of them." Records in Louisiana revealed that no fewer than 1,800 persons were killed, wounded or otherwise injured during the two-week period preceding the 1868 Presidential Election; moreover, fully 3,000 Negroes had been forceably kept away from the polls.

The Ku Klux Klan, declared the report, is a "fearful conspiracy against society. . . . It has demoralized society and held men silent by the terror of its acts and its powers for evil."

Congress outlawed Klan terrorism and authorized the dispatching of Federal troops to put an end to the organization's criminal operations. Less than a year later, Federal commanders were able to report that the Ku Klux Klan had been stamped out completely.

In the last analysis, however, Klan terrorism was not the disease but merely the symptom. The *real* malady was bigotry, that bastard child sired by fear in the womb of weakness. The military forces had been able to snuff out some of the overt manifestations of that bigotry—to strip, as it were, the bastard child of his destructive weapons. But, long after the Klansmen's song had ended, the malady lingered on.

The Beginnings of the Klan

Susan Lawrence Davis

The following selection, first printed in 1924, is an excerpt from Susan Lawrence Davis's *Authentic History: Ku Klux Klan, 1865–1877*. The daughter of a woman who had designed and manufactured regalia for the original Klan, Davis states that her intention is to justify "the men and measures adopted which led to the redemption of the Southern States from Radical, Carpet-bag and Negro rule as was imposed by the Federal Government's reconstruction measures." Here she sympathetically describes how the Ku Klux Klan started out as a form of amusement but eventually developed into a serious fraternal club that used intimidation as a means to control the activities of blacks and northern carpetbaggers.

On December 24, 1865, at Pulaski, Tennessee, there assembled in a small brick building, the law office of Judge Thomas M. Jones, six young men who were soldiers in the Confederate States Army. They had lost all their property, there were no business prospects for them at the time; it was Christmas Eve and their town was saddened not only by the wreckage of Civil War, but by the visitation of a cyclone which had killed and injured many of its inhabitants and destroyed many homes; yet, the spirit of youth could not be conquered in their heroic hearts. One of these young men, Captain John C. Lester, said:

"Boys, let's start something to break this monotony, and to cheer up our mothers and the girls. Let's start a club of some kind."

Excerpted from *Authentic History: Ku Klux Klan, 1865–1877*, by Susan Lawrence Davis (New York, 1924).

The evening was spent in obtaining their object—diversion and amusement. Two committees were appointed to select a name and to prepare a set of rules for the government of the order and the initiation of future members. They then adjourned to meet the following week.

Before the arrival of the next meeting one of the young men, Captain John B. Kennedy, was requested to stay in the home of Col. Thomas Martin, for its protection, while he and his family were absent from Pulaski. Captain Kennedy invited the other organizers of the club, Frank O. McCord, Calvin E. Jones, John C. Lester, Richard R. Reed and James R. Crowe, to meet him there.

HOW THE KLAN GOT ITS NAME

During the evening the organization was perfected. Captain John B. Kennedy, on the committee to select a name mentioned one which he had considered, "Kukloi," from the Greek word "Kuklos," meaning a band or circle. James R. Crowe said "Call it Ku Klux," and no one will know what it means. John C. Lester said: "Add Klan as we are all Scotch-Irish descent."

He then repeated the words: "Ku Klux Klan," the first time these words ever fell from human tongue. The weirdness of the alliteration appealed to the mysterious within them; so the name was adopted with a feeling that they had chosen something which would excite the curiosity of their friends and carry out their idea of amusement, which, most unexpectedly to them, proved a boon to Pulaski and the South.

James R. Crowe suggested to make it more mysterious, that a costume be adopted. They then made a raid upon Mrs. Martin's linen closet and robed themselves with boyish glee in her stiff linen sheets and pillow-cases, as masquerading was a popular form of entertainment in those days. Wishing to make an impression they borrowed some horses from a near-by stable and disguised them with sheets.

They then mounted and rode through the darkness, calling at the homes of their mothers and sweethearts, without speaking a word. They rode slowly through the streets of Pulaski waving to the people and making grotesque gestures, which created merriment to the unsuperstitious, and to the superstitious, great fear.

The next day they heard many favorable comments on the unknown boys who had so paraded, having optimism enough to penetrate the gloom which had settled over this once prosperous and happy community. Aside from the amusement they had created, it was reported on the streets, that many of the idle negroes thought they had seen ghosts from the near-by battle-fields, and had with haste gone back to their former masters, only too willing to work.

The trivial incident of the selection of the ghostly regalia had a most important bearing on the future of the organization. The potency of the name "Ku Klux Klan" was not wholly in the impression made by it on the public, but the members of the Ku Klux Klan themselves first felt its mysterious power, and realized that through this means they might accomplish something towards alleviating the distress then prevalent in their community. Yet their dominant idea was amusement, based on secrecy and mystery.

The one obligation exacted from members was to maintain profound secrecy concerning everything pertaining to the Ku Klux Klan. This obligation prohibited disclosing that they were members of the Ku Klux Klan or giving the name of anyone of them who was a member, and from soliciting members. . . .

RAPID GROWTH

On March 25, 1866, the Ku Klux Klan having increased in numbers, so that they did not wish to meet in the private residence, they established regular headquarters at the home of Dr. Ben. Carter which had been recently wrecked by the cyclone, leaving only three rooms and a large cellar beneath them.

This was on a hill on the outskirts of Pulaski. Around the ruins of this home were the storm-torn trunks of trees which had once been a splendid grove. Now they were like grim, spectre sentinels, making a dreary, desolate uncanny place, but

Why the Klan Was Organized

The following sympathetic portrayal of the first Ku Klux Klan paints the organization as a protective, law-abiding fraternity.

The Ku Klux Klan which was organized following the war between the states was not organized for the purpose, as some have believed, of oppressing and punishing the negroes who had recently been freed and who were as yet unaccustomed to their new circumstances and conditions of life and were as "children crying in the night, children crying for the light and with no language but to cry."

The truth is, the men who composed the membership of the Klan accidently discovered the power their order wielded over the minds of the superstitious negroes, so lately set at liberty, and also over the ignorant and lawless white element, both being rendered unruly by atrocious political influences. These influences and conditions in general called upon the Klan to use this power to protect and defend their helpless and disorganized land. In the beginning this position of Law and Order League had never been remotely anticipated by the members of the order but it was thrust upon them by numerous wanton acts, and the Klan rose as one man to meet the demand, proclaiming with no doubtful voice, that it stood for peace, law and order. That it was not a political or military party, but a protective organization and would "never use violence except in resisting violence."

Mr. and Mrs. W.B. Romine, *A Story of the Original Ku Klux Klan*, 1924.

it was most suitable for the purpose of the Ku Klux Klan as it had the appearance of being haunted and they were by the superstitious believed to be the spirits of the Confederate dead.

This mystery and secrecy of the Ku Klux Klan made a deep impression upon the minds of many men who united with it at this time, and their idea was that they contemplated some great and important mission. This belief caused its rapid growth, though there was not a word in the obligation taken to point out such a conclusion, but the impression grew and the high-sounding titles of the officers and the grotesque dress of its members seemed to them to mean more than mere sport. . . .

THE POWER OF THE MYSTERIOUS

The Ku Klux Klan had gradually realized that the most powerful devices ever constructed for controlling the ignorant and superstitious negroes and carpet-bag politicians, were in their hands. Each day some incident occurred to show the "amazing power of the mysterious over the minds of all classes." These circumstances convinced them that the measures inaugurated for sport only could be used to protect the lives and property of the people of the stricken South.

By a "gentlemen's agreement" throughout the South, no Ku Klux Klans were formed without the consent and co-operation of the six founders who originated the idea, at Pulaski, Tennessee.

At this time most of the eligible men in the town of Pulaski had joined the Ku Klux Klan there, and quite a number from Giles County. Requests were made by these county members to form Klans in their immediate neighborhoods, and while no provision had been made for this expansion, permission was granted, but the strictest injunctions were laid on these men as regards secrecy, mystery, and the high character of the men admitted.

The growth in the country districts was very rapid, and the news that the Ku Klux Klan was growing in numbers, created more sensation than the existence of the Klan itself in Pulaski.

After the County was organized, parades were frequent, and

in their disguises, the Ku Klux Klan would attend meetings being held by the "Carpetbaggers" to incite the negroes and other evil-doers to depredations, and they would circle around these meetings without uttering a word and only making signs, always carrying a torch to light the way which afterwards led to the adoption of the Fiery Cross as their symbol.

CONTROLLING CARPET-BAGGERS AND NEGROES

The first use of the torch to guide the way was by the Pulaski Ku Klux Klan when they went to break up a meeting of carpet-baggers being held in the woods near the "Brick Church" in Giles County. The carpet-baggers were telling the negroes to burn the homes of their former masters and the land would be divided among them.

One faithful negro man was passing this meeting with a sack of meal on his mule taking it to his former master, whom he had never left, and heard the carpet-baggers call the name of his beloved "marster and mistis" as among the victims to be burned alive in their homes that night. He hurried home and told his young master, who was then a member of the Ku Klux Klan, what he had heard.

He left the old negro man to protect his father and mother with the only gun that he had, and hastened to Pulaski where he called together the Ku Klux Klan.

They rode into the meeting from every direction, and so frightened both the negroes and carpet-baggers that they did not stand "on the order of their going," but fled in haste.

They heard of other meetings of like character and spent the rest of the night breaking them up.

The next day many negroes who would not work were found at the plantation gates, appealing for work and protection.

An Interview with General Nathan Bedford Forrest

NATHAN BEDFORD FORREST, INTERVIEWED BY ANONYMOUS

The following piece is an 1868 interview with the first Grand Wizard (national leader) of the Ku Klux Klan, Nathan Bedford Forrest. The interviewer, a traveling correspondent for the *Cincinnati Commercial*, talks with Forrest about reconstruction policies and black suffrage, both of which Forrest opposes. Forrest, a former slave trader and Confederate general, states that he is not a member of the Klan (in keeping with the Klan's policy of secret brotherhood) but praises the group as a "protective, political, military organization." Forrest claims that he is not an "enemy of the negro" and denies charges that Klan members are committing crimes.

Memphis, Tenn., August 28, 1868.
To-day I have enjoyed 'big talks' enough to have gratified any of the famous Indian chiefs who have been treating with General Sherman for the past two years. First I met General N.B. Forrest, then General Gideon A. Pillow, and Governor Isham G. Harris. My first visit was to General Forrest, whom I found at his office, at 8 o'clock this morning, hard at work, although complaining of an illness contracted at the New York convention. The New Yorkers must be a bad set indeed, for I have not met a single delegate from the Southern States who has not been ill ever since he went there. But to General Forrest. Now that the southern people have elevated him to the position of their great leader and oracle, it may not

be amiss to preface my conversation with him with a brief sketch of the gentleman.

I cannot better personally describe him than by borrowing the language of one of his biographers. 'In person he is six feet one inch and a half in height, with broad shoulders, a full chest, and symmetrical, muscular limbs; erect in carriage, and weighs one hundred and eighty-five pounds; dark-gray eyes, dark hair, mustache and beard worn upon the chin; a set of regular white teeth, and clearly cut features; which, altogether, make him rather a handsome man for one forty-seven years of age.

GENERAL FORREST'S BACKGROUND

Previous to the war—in 1852—he left the business of planter, and came to this city and engaged in the business of 'negro trader,' in which traffic he seems to have been quite successful, for, by 1861, he had become the owner of two plantations a few miles below here, in Mississippi, on which he produced about a thousand bales of cotton each year, in the meantime carrying on the negro-trading. In June, 1861, he was authorized by Governor Harris to recruit a regiment of cavalry for the war, which he did, and which was the nucleus around which he gathered the army which he commanded as lieutenant general at the end of the war.

After being seated in his office, I said:

'General Forrest, I came especially to learn your views in regard to the condition of your civil and political affairs in the State of Tennessee, and the South generally. I desire them for publication in the *Cincinnati Commercial*. I do not wish to misinterpret you in the slightest degree, and therefore only ask for such views as you are willing I should publish.'

'I have not now,' he replied, 'and never have had, any opinion on any public or political subject which I would object to having published. I mean what I say, honestly and earnestly, and only object to being misrepresented. I dislike to be placed before the country in a false position, especially as I have not sought the reputation I have gained.'

I replied: 'Sir, I will publish only what you say, and then you can not possibly be misrepresented. Our people desire to know your feelings toward the General Government, the State government of Tennessee, the radical party, both in and out of the State, and upon the question of negro suffrage.'

'Well, sir,' said he, 'when I surrendered my seven thousand men in 1865, I accepted a parole honestly, and I have observed it faithfully up to to-day. I have counseled peace in all the speeches I have made. I have advised my people to submit to the laws of the State, oppressive as they are, and unconstitutional as I believe them to be. I was paroled and not pardoned until the issuance of the last proclamation of general amnesty; and, therefore, did not think it prudent for me to take any active part until the oppression of my people became so great that they could not endure it, and then I would be with them. My friends thought differently, and sent me to New York, and I am glad I went there.'

'Then, I suppose, general, that you think the oppression has become so great that your people should no longer bear it.'

'No,' he answered, 'It is growing worse hourly, yet I have said to the people "Stand fast, let us try to right the wrong by legislation." A few weeks ago I was called to Nashville to counsel with other gentlemen who had been prominently identified with the cause of the confederacy, and we then offered pledges which we thought would be satisfactory to Mr. Brownlow and his legislature, and we told them that, if they would not call out the militia, we would agree to preserve order and see that the laws were enforced. The legislative committee certainly led me to believe that our proposition would be accepted and no militia organized. Believing this, I came home, and advised all of my people to remain peaceful, and to offer no resistance to any reasonable law. It is true that I never have recognized the present government in Tennessee as having any legal existence, yet I was willing to submit to it for a time, with the hope that the wrongs might be righted peaceably.'

'What are your feelings towards the Federal Government, general?'

'I loved the old Government in 1861; I love the Constitution yet. I think it is the best government in the world if administered as it was before the war. I do not hate it; I am opposing now only the radical revolutionists who are trying to destroy it. I believe that party to be composed, as I know it is in Tennessee, of the worst men on God's earth—men who would hesitate at no crime, and who have only one object in view, to enrich themselves.'

'In the event of Governor Brownlow's calling out the militia, do you think there will be any resistance offered to their acts?' I asked.

'That will depend upon circumstances. If the militia are simply called out, and do not interfere with or molest any one, I do not think there will be any fight. If, on the contrary, they do what I believe they will do, commit outrages, or even one outrage, upon the people, they and Mr. Brownlow's government will be swept out of existence; not a radical will be left alive. If the militia are called out, we can not but look upon it as a declaration of war, because Mr. Brownlow has already issued his proclamation directing them to shoot down the Ku Klux wherever they find them; and he calls all southern men Ku Klux.'

'Why, general, we people up north have regarded the Ku Klux as an organization which existed only in the frightened imaginations of a few politicians.'

'Well, sir, there is such an organization, not only in Tennessee but all over the South, and its numbers have not been exaggerated.'

'What are its numbers, general?'

'In Tennessee there are over forty thousand; in all the Southern States about five hundred and fifty thousand men.'

THE NATURE OF THE KU KLUX KLAN

'What is the character of the organization, may I inquire?'

'Yes, sir. It is a protective, political, military organization. I am willing to show any man the constitution of the society. The members are sworn to recognize the Government of the United States. It does not say anything at all about the government of the State of Tennessee. Its objects originally were protection against Loyal Leagues and the Grand Army of the Republic; but after it became general it was found that political matters and interests could best be promoted within it, and it was then made a political organization, giving its support, of course, to the democratic party.'

'But is the organization connected throughout the State?'

'Yes, it is. In each voting precinct there is a captain, who, in addition to his other duties, is required to make out a list of names of men in his precinct, giving all the radicals and all the democrats who are positively known, and showing also the doubtful on both sides and of both colors. This list of names is forwarded to the grand commander of the State, who is thus enabled to know who are our friends and who are not.'

'Can you, or are you at liberty to, give me the name of the commanding officer of this state?'

'No; it would be impolitic.'

'Then I suppose there would be no doubt of a conflict if the militia interfere with the people; is that your view?'

'Yes, sir; if they attempt to carry out Governor Brownlow's proclamation by shooting down Ku Klux—for he calls all southern men Ku Klux—if they go to hunting down and shooting these men, there will be war, and a bloodier one than we have ever witnessed. I have told these radicals here what they might expect in such an event. I have no powder to burn killing negroes. I intend to kill the radicals. I have told them this and more. There is not a radical leader in this town but is a marked man; and if a trouble should break out, not one of them would be left alive. I have told them that they were trying to create a disturbance and then slip out and leave the consequences to fall upon the negro; but they can't do it. Their houses are picketed, and when the fight comes not one of them would ever get out of this town alive. We don't intend they shall ever get out of the country. But I want it distinctly understood that I am opposed to any war, and will only fight in self-defense. If the militia attack us, we will resist to the last; and, if necessary, I think I could raise 40,000 men in five days, ready for the field.'

'Do you think, general, that the Ku Klux have been of any benefit to the State?'

'No doubt of it. Since its organization the leagues have quit killing and murdering our people. There were some foolish young men who put masks on their faces and rode over the country frightening negroes; but orders have been issued to stop that, and it has ceased. You may say further that three members of the Ku Klux have been court-martialed and shot for violations of the orders not to disturb or molest people.'

'Are you a member of the Ku Klux, general?'

'I am not; but am in sympathy and will cooperate with them. I know they are charged with many crimes they are not guilty of. A case in point is the killing of Bierfield at Franklin, a few days ago. I sent a man up there especially to investigate the case, and report to me, and I have his letter here now, in which he states that they had nothing to do with it as an organization.'

ON NEGRO SUFFRAGE

'What do you think of negro suffrage?'

'I am opposed to it under any and all circumstances, and in our convention urged our party not to commit themselves at all upon the subject. If the negroes vote to enfranchise us, I do not think I would favor their disfranchisement. We will stand by those who help us. And here I want you to understand distinctly I am not an enemy to the negro. We want him here among us; he is the only laboring class we have; and, more than that, I would sooner trust him than the white scalawag or carpetbagger. When I entered the army I took forty-seven negroes into the army with me, and forty-five of them were surrendered with me. I said to them at the start: "This fight is against slavery; if we lose it, you will be made free; if we whip the fight, and you stay with me and be good boys, I will set you free; in either case you will be free." These boys stayed with me, drove my teams, and better confederates did not live.'

'Do you think the Ku Klux will try to intimidate the negroes at the election?'

'I do not think they will. Why, I made a speech at Browns-ville the other day, and while there a lieutenant who served with me came to me and informed me that a band of radicals had been going through the country claiming to be Ku Klux, and disarming the negroes, and then selling their arms. I told him to have the matter investigated, and, if true, to have the parties arrested.' . . .

ON GENERAL GRANT

'What do you think of General Grant?' I asked.

'I regard him as a great military commander, a good man, honest and liberal, and if elected will, I hope and believe, exe-cute the laws honestly and faithfully. And by the way, a report has been published in some of the newspapers, stating that while General Grant and lady were at Corinth, in 1862, they took and carried off furniture and other property. I here brand the author as a liar. I was at Corinth only a short time ago, and I personally investigated the whole matter, talked with the people with whom he and his lady lived while there, and they say that their conduct was everything that could be expected of a gentleman and lady, and deserving the highest praise. I am opposed to Gen-eral Grant in everything, but I would do him justice.'

The foregoing is the principal part of my conversation with the general. I give the conversation, and leave the reader to form his own opinion as to what General Forrest means to do. I think he has been so plain in his talk that it can not be mis-understood.

The Klan and Womanhood

KATHLEEN M. BLEE

In the following selection, Kathleen M. Blee discusses why the no-tion of threatened white womanhood was especially significant to the first Ku Klux Klan. In the post–Civil War South, many whites feared that newly freed black men would retaliate against their for-mer masters by sexually assaulting white women. The Klan capital-ized on these fears; furthermore, the alleged threats to white woman-hood came to symbolize the reconstruction era's perceived threat to Southern white culture and manhood. Klan members attempted to reassert their sense of masculine authority and racial and cultural su-premacy by torturing black men and raping black women. Blee is the author of *Women of the Klan*, from which this selection is excerpted.

From the beginning, the rituals and organized terrorism of the first KKK were based on symbols of violent white masculinity and vulnerable white femininity. When the KKK was organized in Tennessee immediately after the Civil War, it summoned defeated sons of the Confederacy to defend the principles of white supremacy against interference by North-erners and retaliation by freed black slaves. As it grew from a prankish club of dejected soldiers to a loosely knit and highly secret vigilante terrorist network in the defeated Southern states, the Klan continued to merge ideas of sexual menace with those of racial and political danger.[1]

During the late 1860s the Klan spread its reign of terror throughout Southern and border states. Gangs of Klansmen threatened, flogged, and murdered countless black and white women and men. But the Klan's violence was not arbitrary. It

Excerpted from *Women of the Klan: Racism and Gender in the 1920s*, by Kathleen M. Blee (Los Angeles: University of California Press, 1991). Copyright © 1991 by the University of California Press. Reprinted with permission.

applied terror to bolster the crumbling foundations of Southern supremacy against political inroads by blacks, Republicans, and Northern whites. Schoolteachers, revenue collectors, election officials, and Republican officeholders—those most involved with dismantling parts of the racial state—as well as all black persons, were the most common targets of Klan terror.[2] The KKK was particularly expert in the use of sexual violence and brutality. Klan mobs humiliated white Southern Republicans ("scalawags") by sexually abusing them. Klansmen routinely raped and sexually tortured women, especially black women, during "kluxing" raids on their households. Widely reported acts of lynching, torture, and sexual mutilation intimidated Klan opponents and terrorized its enemies.[3]

The secrecy and juvenile rituals of the early KKK borrowed heavily from the long tradition of male fraternal societies. Men bound themselves to one another through allegiances of race, gender, and a shared desire to preserve the racial state of the South in the face of military defeat. Even the Klan's name, derived from the Greek *kuklos* (circle), reinforced its quest for white male commonality across divisions of social class and local status.[4] Although the Klan's politics would become fervently anti-Catholic over time, the first Klan created a culture whose costumes and secret ritual mimicked the symbolism and ritual of the male-based hierarchy of the Roman Catholic church. It barred white women (and all nonwhites) from membership, just as the Southern polity did. If the abuse and exclusion of blacks reinforced an ethos of racial power, strength, and invulnerability among the fraternity of white Klansmen so, too, the exclusion of white women served to celebrate and solidify the masculinity of racial politics.[5]

IMPERILED WHITE WOMANHOOD

Although women did not participate openly in the actions of the first KKK, the idea of "white womanhood" was a crucial rallying point for postbellum Klan violence. Klansmen insisted that white women benefited from the Southern racial state, even as strict gender hierarchies within white society ensured that women would not be consulted on this matter. In an appearance in 1871 before the U.S. Senate, Nathan Bedford Forrest, the first Grand Wizard, argued that the Klan was needed because Southern whites faced great insecurity. He pointed dramatically at a situation in which "ladies were ravished by some of these negroes, who were tried and put in the penitentiary, but were turned out in a few days afterward."[6]

This theme of imperiled Southern white womanhood echoed throughout writings by the first KKK and its apologists. White women, especially widows living alone on isolated plantations, were highly visible symbols through which the Klan could rouse public fears that blacks' retaliation against their former white masters would be exacted upon white daughters, wives, and mothers. Without the Klan, white men were powerless to assist white women who faced frightful sexual violations by newly freed black men:

> We note the smile of helpless masculinity give but feebly assuring answer to its mate's frown of distressful inquiry, as the sullen roll of the drum and the beastly roar of the savage rasp the chords of racial instinct. As we watch the noble countenance of modest, innocent Southern maidenhood pale into death-defying scorn, as she contemplates the hellish design of the black brute in human form.[7]

Women were symbols for the first KKK in another way. The feared assault on white women not only threatened white men's sexual prerogatives but symbolized the rape of the Southern racial state in the Reconstruction era as well. In *Hooded Americanism,* David Chalmers notes the double meaning of white womanhood for white men in the antebellum and immediate postbellum South:

> [White womanhood] not only stood at the core of his sense of property and chivalry, she represented the heart of his culture. By the fact that she was not accessible to the Negro, she marked the ultimate line of difference between white and black . . . it was impossible to assault either the

Southern woman or the South without having implicitly levied carnal attacks on the other.[8]

THE COMPLEXITY OF SEXUAL SYMBOLISM

The complexity of gender and sexual symbolism in the first Klan shows also in the propaganda circulated among and by Klansmen. Klansmen saw the abolition of slavery both as the loss of sexual access to black women and as the potential loss of exclusive sexual access to white women. An enfranchised black man, the Klan insisted, "considered freedom synonymous with equality and his greatest ambition was to marry a white wife." Klan propaganda steadfastly portrayed women as passive sexual acquisitions of men and insisted that black men used physical coercion to wrest sexual favors (and even marriage vows) from white female victims. Underlying this message, however, was the concern that, given free choice among male sexual partners, at least some white women might choose black men. As a threat to the racial and sexual privileges of white men in the postbellum South, black husbands nearly equaled black rapists of white women.[9]

All histories of the first Klan emphasize that the success of the Klan depended on images of rape and miscegenation between white women and black men. Accounts that lack a feminist-informed analysis, however, miss some of the political significance of references to actual and symbolic rape and miscegenation. In *The Fiery Cross,* for example, Wyn Craig Wade argues that slavery corrupted sexual relations between white men and white women. Placed on a pedestal in antebellum Southern society, white women became "like statues in bed," as Wade remarks, sexually inaccessible to white men. In response white men turned to powerless black female slaves, to "release the passion they were unable to experience with their wives." As the Confederacy crumbled, white men feared that black men would retaliate in like manner by sexually assaulting now vulnerable white mothers, daughters, sisters, and wives.[10]

The interpretation of rape and miscegenation given in *The Fiery Cross*—one shared by most histories of the Klan—presents images of interracial sexuality in the postbellum South as a battle among groups of men divided along racial, class, and regional lines. As men struggled to preserve or challenge a racial caste system, all women were reduced to a common function as political symbols—symbols of racial privilege or subordination, regional self-determination or subjugation. This interpretation superposes hierarchies of gender on the greater cleavages of race and class in Southern society.

A QUESTION OF POWER

A feminist analysis differently interprets the images of rape, gender, and sexuality in the first Klan. Modern feminist scholarship considers rape to be foremost an issue of power, not sexual desire. The Klan's call to defend white women against rape by black men signified a relation of power between men and women as well as between white and black men. On one level, the Klan's emphasis on the rape threat that white women faced was a message about the sexual violation of women by men. Underlying this level, however, was a deeper threat to white men's sexual privileges. As Catherine MacKinnon argues, "the definitive element of rape centers around male-defined loss, not coincidentally also upon the way men define loss of exclusive access."[11]

Rape was a volatile issue in both antebellum and postbellum Southern society divided by race and gender. The racial state of the slave South, like the racialist state that followed the Civil War, was built on a foundation that dictated a hierarchical division of male and female, as well as white and black. It kept white women within a role that was exalted in prose but sharply divided from and inferior to the privileged social role of white men. White men monopolized rights to property and the franchise and dictated the rules by which their wives, children, slaves, servants, and hired labor would live. Social privileges were formed along overlapping hierarchies of race, gender, and social class. Political, economic, and social power were reserved for white men, especially propertied white men.[12]

Within this context of hierarchies in Southern society we

must imagine the mobilizing power of interracial sexual issues for the Ku Klux Klan. The Klan avowed horror of miscegenation but practiced it, as did antebellum white plantation masters, as a tactic of terror. Too, the Klan characterized rape equally as a metaphor for Southern white male disempowerment and as an atrocity committed against women. We cannot reduce this complex symbolic layering of race, sexuality, and gender in the language and the political practice of the Ku Klux Klan to a collective manifestation of psychosexual frustration, repression, and fear by white Southern men. Rather, we must analyze the massive social movement of the first KKK in the context of long-standing cleavages underlying Southern society.[13]

MASCULINE WHITE SUPREMACY

In these hierarchies of Reconstruction-era Southern states, black men were a threat to white men's sexual access to women (both black and white). Sexual torture and emasculation of black men by mobs of Klansmen validated the claim that masculinity ("real manhood") was the exclusive prerogative of white men. The rape of black women by white Klansmen represented the Klan's symbolic emasculation of black men through violating "their" women while affirming the use of male sexuality as a weapon of power against women.[14] Southern women, white and black, occupied a symbolic terrain on which white men defended their racial privileges. The symbols of white female vulnerability and white masculine potency took power equally from beliefs in masculine and in white supremacy.

The first Klan movement collapsed quickly. Despite an elaborate hierarchy, the Klan lacked direction and political focus. By the late 1860s many local Klan units became chaotic unorganized gangs of terrorists; the federal government intensified its military and political control of the Southern states. In 1870 the Grand Wizard ordered the organization dissolved, insisting that atrocities blamed on the Klan were in fact committed by opportunistic nonmembers. The remaining local remnants of the first Ku Klux Klan disintegrated during the mid-1870s.[15]

NOTES

1. Walter L. Fleming, "The Prescript of the Ku Klux Klan," *Southern Historical Association* 7 (September 1903): 327–48; David Annan, "The Ku Klux Klan," in *Secret Societies,* ed. Norman MacKenzie (Holt, Rinehart and Winston, 1967); Mecklin, *The Ku Klux Klan.*

2. Joint Select Committee on the Condition of Affairs in the Late Insurrectionary States, *Affairs in the Late Insurrectionary States,* 42d Cong., 2d sess., 1872 (reprint, Arno Press, 1969); Seymour Martin Lipset, "An Anatomy of the Klan," *Commentary* 40 (October 1965): 74–83; Frank Tannenbaum, "The Ku Klux Klan: Its Social Origin in the South," *Century Magazine* 105 (April 1923): 873–83; Wade, *The Fiery Cross,* 31–80.

3. Jacquelyn Dowd Hall, "'The Mind that Burns in Each Body': Women, Rape, and Racial Violence," in *Powers of Desire: The Politics of Sexuality,* ed. Ann Snitow, Christine Stansell, and Sharon Thompson (Monthly Review Press, 1983); Wade, *The Fiery Cross,* 54–79; Frank Tannenbaum, *Darker Phases of the South* (Negro Universities Press, 1924), 33–34. The Klan's unintended advertisement of sex parallels that of the social purity movement of the late nineteenth and early twentieth centuries, as described by David Pivar, *Purity Crusade* (Greenwood Press, 1973), and also the moral reform movement of the mid–nineteenth century, analyzed by Carroll Smith-Rosenberg, *Disorderly Conduct: Visions of Gender in Victorian America* (Oxford University Press, 1986), 109–28.

4. Despite the common stereotype of the first Klan as composed primarily of lower-class Southern whites, men in the professions and business were active also (Wade, *The Fiery Cross,* 31–80; David Bennett, *The Party of Fear: From Nativist Movements to The New Right in American History* [University of North Carolina Press, 1988]).

5. Jacquelyn Dowd Hall, *Revolt Against Chivalry: Jesse Daniel Ames and the Women's Campaign Against Lynching* (Columbia University Press, 1979); Jacquelyn Dowd Hall, "'A Truly Subversive Affair': Women Against Lynching in the Twentieth-Century South," in *Women of America: A History,* ed. Carol Berkin and Mary Beth Norton (Houghton Mifflin, 1979); Elizabeth Fox-Genovese, *Within the Plantation Household: Black and White Women of the Old South* (University of North Carolina Press, 1988), esp. 37–70; see also Laurence Alan Baughman, *Southern Rape Complex: A Hundred-Year Psychosis* (Pendulum, 1966), 176–77.

6. Annan, "Ku Klux Klan."

7. Fleming, "Prescript," 10; see also Winfield Jones, *Knights of the Ku Klux Klan* (Tocsin, 1941), 98. Annie Cooper Burton, president of a chapter of the United Daughters of the Confederacy, wrote *The Ku Klux Klan* (Warren T. Potter, 1916) with thanks to the Klan and included an interview with Captain H. W. Head, former Klan Grand Cyclops of Nashville. Peter Stearns suggests that the nineteenth-century creation of an ideology of white female

vulnerability was in part a response to the changing image of manhood in an industrial society (*Be a Man!* [Holmes and Meier, 1979]).

8. Baughman, *Southern Rape Complex,* 176–77; Chalmers, *Hooded Americanism,* 21.

9. S.E.F. Rose, *The Ku Klux Klan or the Invisible Empire* (L. Graham, 1914),17.

10. Wade, *The Fiery Cross,* 20.

11. Catherine A. MacKinnon, "Feminism, Marxism, Method, and State," *Signs* 6 (March 1983): 30.

12. Fox-Genovese, *Plantation Household,* esp. 37–99.

13. This analysis assumes that collective frustration and structural positions cannot explain the development of social movements in the absence of shared resources and a common worldview. See Sara Evans, *Personal Politics;* and Charles Tilly, *From Mobilization to Revolution* (Addison-Wesley, 1973).

14. Hall, " 'The Mind' "; see also Tannenbaum, *Darker Phases,* 31–33.

15. *Affairs in the Late Insurrectionary States;* Fleming, "Prescript"; Annan, "Ku Klux Klan."

CHAPTER 2

THE EARLY TWENTIETH CENTURY KLAN

AMERICAN
SOCIAL
MOVEMENTS

The Ku Klux Klan Revived

WILLIAM PEIRCE RANDEL

The twentieth-century Ku Klux Klan began in 1915 as a fraternal organization that claimed to support morality, Christianity, law and order, and patriotic Americanism, writes William Peirce Randel in the following selection. By the early 1920s this revived Klan determined that the foes of America included not just blacks, but Jews, Catholics, immigrants, and those who denounced the ideal of white supremacy. While the Klan publicly denied that it was anti-minority, Klan leaders drew new members by capitalizing on the public indignation caused by news reports about crimes committed by minorities, notes Randel. The organization became financially successful and politically prominent, influencing several state elections throughout the 1920s. Randel, a professor of English and American Studies, is the author of *The Ku Klux Klan: A Century of Infamy*.

The twentieth-century Klan began as the dream-child of a lanky Alabamian named William Joseph Simmons. At different times in his life—he was born in 1882—he had been a probationary Methodist preacher and a traveling salesman; and he may have taught American history, briefly, at Lanier University, a small college in Atlanta that the Klan later owned. The one enduring passion of his life was fraternalism. "I believe in fraternal orders," he once asserted, "and fraternal associations among men." He proved it by joining a dozen or more Masonic orders and the Woodmen of the World. His nights were filled with lodge meetings. As leader of the Woodmen's drill team he picked up the title of "Colonel."

In 1911, while convalescing in a hospital after a serious au-

Excerpted from *The Ku Klux Klan: A Century of Infamy*, by William Peirce Randel (Philadelphia: Chilton Books, 1965). Copyright © 1965 by Cahners. Reprinted with permission.

tomobile accident, Simmons had plenty of time to review his life. As he later reminisced, it was then that his fondest boyhood dream—reviving the old Ku Klux Klan—returned with compelling urgency. His father had been a Klansman; and his Negro "mammy" had often regaled him with exciting Klan stories. A new Klan would raise American fraternalism to heights never achieved before. . . .

A REINCARNATED KLAN

After dark on Thanksgiving Day of 1915 Simmons led fifteen followers to the top of Stone Mountain, east of Atlanta, for the first initiation ceremony of what he called the "reincarnated Klan." It was not greatly different from the ritual devised at Pulaski, Tennessee, back in 1866. On an altar—a projecting bit of rock—were placed an American flag, an open Bible, an unsheathed sword, and a canteen of water. (Later on, "initiation water," scooped from the Chattahoochee River near Atlanta and sold for ten dollars a quart, was one of several lucrative sources of income for Simmons and his successors as Grand Wizard.) The one striking innovation on Stone Mountain was the erection and burning of a cross, the only source of light—and warmth—for the shivering original Knights of the modern Klan.

A week later Simmons incorporated the organization in Fulton County (Atlanta), which has remained to this day a hub of Klan activity. The old Klan had never sought the legal recognition that incorporation represents; its leaders, who put all their reliance on total secrecy, would have been aghast at the very idea. But from the outset Simmons conceived of an organization well protected by legal status, as widely publicized as possible, and amply productive of income—for himself.

A tall, slender man whose pince-nez glasses provided a certain air of distinction, Simmons was an effective public speaker; but, though crowds enjoyed his spellbinding elocution, he enlisted new members at a very disappointing rate. The war in Europe was a formidable rival for interest. By the time the United States entered the war in 1917, the Klan had fewer than two thousand members, mostly in Georgia and Alabama, enough to issue a public denunciation of a shipyard strike in Mobile and to march in a reunion parade of Confederate veterans, but not nearly enough to attract more than local attention. To make matters worse, an assistant absconded with what there was in the treasury, and Simmons had to mortgage his home to keep the Klan alive. Those were lean days, but Simmons had unquenchable faith in his dream-child.

THE KLAN'S NEW MANAGERS

A residue of idealism kept Simmons from accepting offers made by men solely interested in profit and woefully indifferent to the spirit of true fraternalism. But in 1920, after four years and more of discouragement, he finally gave in; the promise of $100 a week for life was too attractive to resist. The day he signed the contract, June 7, 1920, marks the real beginning of the Klan as it flourished and became a national byword.

The offer that Simmons could not resist was made by Edward Young Clarke, a onetime newspaperman who, during the war, had gained a certain proficiency in directing patriotic fund-raising campaigns. In the course of organizing a Harvest Festival in Atlanta, Clarke had met an engaging widow, Mrs. Elizabeth Tyler, who not only shared his opinion that the public existed to be fleeced but who also had some money of her own—quite a lot of it, in fact. The two formed a Southern Publicity Association and raised money for such groups as the YMCA, the YWCA, and the Salvation Army. Hungry for bigger things, they saw an untapped potential in the Klan. Colonel Simmons had all the qualities of an ideal front man; he had only to consent to let them manage the Klan's entire operation.

Everybody had some knowledge of the Reconstruction Klan, however hazy, if only from *The Birth of a Nation,* first shown in 1915 and one of the great successes of moving picture history. One writer intimates that seeing it gave Simmons the idea of reviving the Klan. If any film has ever been a stimulus to intolerance, this one certainly was. Its effect on the mass audience was to provide a kind of sanction for hate feelings and to glamorize secret societies devoted to preserving race distinctions and to resisting central government. Once the Klan was available, it would seem likely that men would hasten to join it—the kind of men, at least, who wanted some release for their frustrations.

But Simmons was a little too prone to stress the fraternal side of his Klan and to underplay the appeal to intolerance. Furthermore, racial antagonism was, at the moment, too slight to be a good lever for recruitment. Once Clarke and Mrs. Tyler took over, they studied the situation with the critical eyes of professional publicists and decided that the growing popular concern over postwar morals was the thing to manipulate. They devised a propaganda campaign to create an image of the Klan as a guardian of public morality. Using Colonel Simmons as mouthpiece, they made a great show of endorsing and supporting worthy causes of every kind. Early in the life of the old Klan certain devices had proved very effective, such as asking an illiterate Negro to "hold my head for awhile," and handing him a gourd that resembled a head. The comparable effective gimmick of the new Klan was a column of Klansmen in full regalia marching down a church aisle during a service, depositing a donation on the communion table, and marching out—all in perfect silence. Who could oppose an organization so obviously devoted to good clean living and to encouraging all that was best in American life?

TRUE AMERICANISM

Meanwhile it was important to identify the enemies of true Americanism. It was absurdly easy to point them out: all the recent immigrants from odd corners of Europe who exhibited no fondness for Anglo-Saxon tradition and resisted quick assimilation, even choosing to stay in congested city slums and, by their very presence, to make the big cities more sinful and un-American than ever. (Our historic agrarianism played a part here; in Klan thinking, village and farm people were the best variety of Americans.) And then there were the readily identifiable minorities, especially the Jews and the

Catholics, the former allegedly incapable of assimilation and intent only on getting rich fast, and the latter notorious for their allegiance to the Pope. . . .

The ten questions put to all would-be Klansmen illustrate the concept of true Americanism that the modern Klan sought to establish:

1. Is the motive prompting your ambition to be a Klansman serious and unselfish?
2. Are you a native-born white, Gentile, American citizen?
3. Are you absolutely opposed to and free of any allegiance of any nature to any cause, government, people, sect or ruler that is foreign to the U.S.A.?
4. Do you believe in the tenets of the Christian religion?
5. Do you esteem the U.S.A. and its institutions above any other government, civil, political, or ecclesiastical in the whole world?
6. Will you, without mental reservation, take a solemn oath to defend, preserve, and enforce same?
7. Do you believe in clanishness [sic] and will you faithfully practice same toward Klansmen?
8. Do you believe in and will you faithfully strive for the eternal maintenance of white supremacy?
9. Will you faithfully obey our constitution and laws, and conform willingly to all our usages, requirements, and regulations?
10. Can you always be depended on?

The years 1921 through 1926 produced a remarkable number of books and pamphlets attacking and defending the Klan. In the pro-Klan books can be found a systematic analysis of the points made in these initiation questions, sometimes even chapter by chapter. . . . Colonel Winfield Jones's *Story of the Ku Klux Klan* (1921) and a later abridged version called *Knights of the Ku Klux Klan* (1941) took up the test questions one by one. The *Story*, appearing so soon after Clarke and Mrs. Tyler assumed control of the Klan, was timely in the extreme. Jones said he was not a Klansman, and that Colonel Simmons had

given him access to the Klan records only "with great reluctance," but this may have been a dodge to make the book look
like the objective appraisal of an outsider. The revision, twenty
years later, was published by the Tocsin Press, owned by an arch
Klansman named E.N. Sanctuary, composer of Klan songs.
Jones closed the *Story* with an optimistic prediction:

> The Anglo-Saxon is the typeman of history. To him must
> yield the self-centered Hebrew, the cultured Greek, the vir-
> ile Roman, the mystic Oriental. The Psalmist must have
> had him in mind when he struck his soundless harp and
> sang: "O Lord; thou hast made him a little lower than the
> angels, and hast crowned him with glory and honor. Thou
> hast made him to have dominion over the works of thy
> hands; thou hast put all things under his feet." The Ku Klux
> Klan desires that its ruling members shall be of this all-
> conquering blood. . . . The Ku Klux Klan was planned for
> the white American.

In brief, the Ku Klux Klan desires to be, hopes to be, plans
to be, and will be a great, influential, helpful, patriotic,
American fraternal order, taking its allotted place with similar secret brotherhoods, and with them working out our
Christian civilization, adding to the gifts and graces, the
prosperity and happiness of mankind, and standing for the
noble, the true and the good, for the majesty of law, for the
advancement of the human race.

RELIGIOUS PREJUDICE AND NATIVISM

The Ku Klux Klan Under the Searchlight by Leroy A. Curry, and
K.K.K. Friend or Foe: Which? by Blaine Mast, both appeared in
1924, a banner Klan year. Curry deemed the Klan essential for
reviving true Americanism and its Christian base, and praised
it for fighting all forces that threatened to undermine the solid
old American principles. His favorite phrase was "this great
American Organization." Blaine Mast described Jews as
shrewd rich lechers, luring Gentile girls into joyrides and then
into hotel rooms; but he added that Jews weren't the only sin-
ners in America. One of his most interesting passages refers to

the Catholic conspiracy, but could be taken in quite another sense by an unsympathetic reader: "A nation's greatest enemy is never without—*It is always within!* The worse political enemy is he who stirs up civil strife, as witness our Civil War in 1861-1865." A religious war, he added, would make the Civil War seem mild; "intolerant, lop-sided, radical leaders are never safe to follow."

The Klan, by inference, offered leadership that was safe. . . .

Except for the eighth test question on the preservation of white supremacy, the new Klan sounds less like the "reincarnation" of the old Klan that Colonel Simmons liked to talk about than a recrudescence of the nativism that has been a virtual constant in American history. Each great wave of fresh immigration has been followed by a reaction, most notably the Know-Nothing movement just before the Civil War and the A.P.A.—the American Protective Association—at the end of the nineteenth century. Both of these were particularly opposed to Catholics. The Know-Nothings, alarmed by the propensity of Irish Catholics to enter politics, sought deliberately to bar all foreigners, especially Catholics, from running for office. . . .

The A.P.A. was more recent in memory. It began in the further Midwest—Iowa, Kansas, Nebraska—and it was deliberately encouraged by forgeries of Catholic documents. In whole counties Protestant families kept their guns loaded and barricaded their houses. The A.P.A. evolved into a political pressure group, but what most of its scattered rural members remembered was the threat of overt violence—specifically the alleged Catholic plot to massacre all Protestants. Many of these Protestants were of recent migration, people whose own experience in the Old Country had included actual religious persecution. Americans longer in the land were less susceptible; they had a greater sense of security and of belonging.

Where the bulk of the population had been long in the land, the Klan capitalized on the fear of subverted customs; where everybody was of recent migration, the Klan concentrated on threats to their acceptance. In much the same way, a little later, the Klan could be Republican in Ohio and Democratic in Mississippi in its effort to gain political power.

In both the old Klan and the new, wide discrepancies can readily be detected between stated purposes and actual practice. The rank-and-file members could only judge by what the leaders handed out; and since the copy was skillfully prepared, it sounded fine. Ed Clarke and Bessie Tyler kept a sharp eye on the current news, waiting for events they could turn to their own purposes. Foul murders by white Protestants could be ignored; a foul murder by a member of an un-American minority could be seized upon to rouse public indignation and to draw new members to the Klan, which never stopped declaring its endorsement of law and order. . . .

BIG BUSINESS

The Klan records show deposits in many different banks, sometimes in checking and savings accounts, sometimes in safe deposit boxes, and sometimes, although it violated the law governing the use and control of trust funds, in the personal accounts of individuals. It has been estimated that by 1925 six million Americans had joined and paid the ten-dollar Klecktoken. Counting the sales of regalia and "initiation water," something like $75,000,000 was paid into the Order by the members. The Klan was big business. Its litigation alone approached the $10 million mark. It should not be astonishing, incidentally, that Ed Clarke, always canny, forced the Klan attorneys to split with him the fees they charged to defend Klansmen who got into trouble with the law.

It was acutely embarrassing to Simmons when, in 1922, one of his oldest Klan friends, Imperial Kligrapp (Secretary) Wade, charged in a lawsuit that Simmons was more often drunk than sober and that Clarke was the real leader of the Klan. This may have prompted Simmons to ask Clarke to find him a personal assistant. The man Clarke chose was a Dallas dentist, Hiram Wesley Evans, who had made quite a name for himself in Texas Klan circles. He was given the title of Grand Dragon. Then Simmons made the mistake of taking a six-month leave of absence, and, while he was absent, Evans maneuvered himself into power.

When Simmons returned, he summoned a Klonvokation on November 27, 1922. He assumed he would be re-elected Grand Wizard, and proposed for Evans the new title of Emperor. But he was no match for the sharp-minded men around him. At four o'clock one morning he was awakened by Grand Dragon [D.C.] Stephenson, of Indiana, and Fred Savage, head of the Klan's fifty-man secret police force. They warned him that if he let his name be offered for reelection, his character would be violently attacked on the floor, something the Klan could not afford to let happen. Stephenson and Savage apparently represented a group of Klan officials, mostly Grand Dragons, who were sick and tired of control by Simmons, Clarke, and Bessie Tyler. They badgered Simmons into naming Evans as his successor, and he did just that at the Klonvokation. All he could salvage for himself was the title of Emperor which he had suggested for Evans.

From the Klan point of view, Evans was an improvement over both Clarke and Simmons. A Vanderbilt graduate, he had been reasonably successful as a dentist, and he had none of the conspicuous vices of Simmons. He dressed well and was a good public speaker. He had a much better sense of the groups in America with interests parallel to those of the Klan, especially large corporations. And he recognized that Clarke was no Klansman at heart. He at least shared with Simmons the dedication to fraternalism. . . .

BUILDING POLITICAL POWER

Evans made numerous changes. In respect to organization, the most significant change was putting all officials on salary. But of greater importance was his stepped-up campaign to give Klansmen their money's worth by making the Klan a force in politics. He apparently hoped to elect enough Klansmen to control Congress and even the White House. As groundwork for these ambitious plans he sought to win favor with the nation's Protestant clergymen and to develop a nation-wide pattern of sympathetic journalism.

Money was no problem. It was a simple matter to send a $50,000 check to support a pro-Klan candidate in some election, or even to take $25,000 in bills along with him on a trip, for personal distribution, if this seemed expedient. Money was lavished on periodicals. *Dawn,* published in Chicago, *The Fellowship Forum* in Washington, *The Searchlight* in Georgia, *The Fiery Cross,* and *The One Hundred Percent American* were among the best-known of the Klan periodicals, though some of them took pains to conceal the Klan support. E.N. Sanctuary's Tocsin Press in New York, meanwhile, was virtually a Klan publishing house.

Champion of Protestantism that it claimed to be, it was essential for the Klan to seek the support of Protestant clergy, or at least to minimize clerical criticism. Simply by not protesting when robed Klansmen marched into churches with donations, clergymen tacitly gave approval; it might have been difficult to order the column to leave. Besides, money is money, whatever its source.

Some Protestant leaders did speak out, however, against the Klan. Three at least, and no doubt others, were so strong in their denunciation that the Klan took countermeasures in the hope of discrediting them. Dr. C.B. Wilmer, of the Protestant Episcopal Church in Atlanta, was investigated in two states by police officers in an effort to ruin his career. Dr. Plato Durham, a Methodist minister and a professor at Emory University outside Atlanta, was branded a Negrophile by the Klan. Ashby Jones, Baptist, was publicly slandered for his opposition to the Klan's anti-Negro measures; that he happened to be the son of J. William Jones, Robert E. Lee's chaplain and eventual biographer, did not make him immune from Klan attack. . . .

SUSPICION OF INTELLECTUALS

It is tempting to suppose that the average intelligence of Klan members was low; what else could explain their willingness to contribute good money to an organization that gave them nothing in return (except a chance to hate)? Wizard Evans virtually admitted in an article that his followers were relatively simple, motivated more by emotion than by reason; the passage illustrates a recurring popular suspicion of intellectuals, though in those days he didn't have the term "egg-head" at his disposal:

> We are a movement of the plain people, very weak in the matter of culture, intellectual support, and trained leadership. We are demanding, and we expect to win, a return of power into the hands of the everyday, not highly cultured, not overly intellectualized, but unspoiled and not de-Americanized, average citizen of the old stock. Our members and leaders are all of this class—the opposition of the intellectuals and liberals who hold the leadership and from whom we expect to wrest control, is almost automatic.

> This is undoubtedly a weakness. It lays us open to the charge of being "hicks" and "rubes" and "drivers of second-hand Fords." We admit it. Far worse, it makes it hard for us to state our case and advocate our crusade in the most effective way, for most of us lack skill in language. . . .

> Every popular movement has suffered from just this handicap. . . .

> The Klan does not believe that the fact that it is emotional and instinctive, rather than coldly intellectual, is a weakness. All action comes from emotion, rather than from ratiocination. Our emotions and the instincts on which they are based have been bred into us for thousands of years; far longer than reason has had a place in the human brain. . . . They are the foundations of our American civilization, even more than our great historic documents; they can be trusted where the fine-haired reasoning of the denatured intellectuals cannot.

The article containing these candid statements appeared in *The North American Review* in the spring of 1926, a time when the Klan had begun to lose its momentum.

Our Vanishing People

WILLIAM JOSEPH SIMMONS

William Joseph Simmons, the first Grand Wizard of the revived Ku Klux Klan, warns that growing numbers of immigrants and blacks will overtake the white, native-born American population. It is the Klan's intention, Simmons explains, to protect the white race from extinction and to preserve the honor and glory of Anglo-Saxon American civilization. This selection is excerpted from Simmons's 1924 book, *The Klan Unmasked.*

We Americans are nothing if not humanitarian. We have in the United States many varieties of organization for the assistance of the various foreign racial and national groups upon our soil. We have also done not a little for the succor of the peoples of the old world who are now in such great distress. The larger humanitarian motive is as a guiding star to millions of Americans. It leads them and lights their way. To many such it may seem unnecessary, to some preposterous, for the organization of which I have the honor to be chief to be founded and developed. But a sober second thought is required here. Let us grant that a people which, in its weakness, faces permanent injury, requires help that it may survive and grow. Then indeed, it follows that we Americans, as a people, need to help ourselves first of all. *As a people and a nation we are face to face with dissolution.* In the Ku Klux Klan we have an institution designed to help in the stupendous task of saving ourselves from failing and falling.

Excerpted from *The Klan Unmasked*, by William Joseph Simmons (Atlanta: W.E. Thompson Publishing Company, 1924).

THE AMERICAN PEOPLE FACE EXTINCTION

We Americans as a peculiar people face extinction upon our own soil. Let me be fully understood. I do not wish in the least to appear sensational. I wish only to state a few simple facts which should be apparent to any American who investigates, ever so briefly, the true condition of his country. So often, during the past twenty-two years, I have been oppressed in heart as I have seen how little public interest this crucial matter has aroused. If my tendency has, at times, been somewhat pessimistic and fearful, I claim that there is cause enough for fear and pessimism. Surely there is great need that intensest sadness and sorrow strike deep into the hearts of Americans, if we are now to help ourselves and live.

We Americans are a perishing people. From the point of view of history we are being wiped from the face of the earth with a rapidity which almost staggers hope. First let me clearly define what I mean by the phrase, "We American People." I mean by that phrase those white, native-born citizens of this country whose ancestry, birth and training has been such as to give them to-day a full share in the basic principles, the ideals and the practice of our American civilization. I do not mean that a foreign-born citizen can not be a good citizen. On the contrary, many of our foreign-born are excellent citizens. Yet I most positively mean what the title at the head of this chapter distinctly suggests. We, the American people, we whose breed fought through the Revolutionary War and the War Between the States, the people by whose courage the great American wilderness was penetrated, and by whose painstaking industry that wilderness was subjugated and made fruitful—that this people, who gave to the world Washington and Franklin, Jefferson and Hamilton, Andrew Jackson and Daniel Webster, Robert E. Lee and Abraham Lincoln—this people, our people, is on the downward way to the early ending of its remarkable history. The mighty length and breadth of the soil made sacred by our struggles and our victories is now being given over, with ever greater rapidity, to various peoples of a totally different mold. I am not saying that these other peoples are bad in character or in any way unworthy. May Heaven witness for my colleagues and myself of the Ku Klux Klan that we bear them no ill will whatsoever. I hope that none of us as individuals or as an organization may do them aught but good. We wish, above all, to be moved in all things by that Christian spirit upon which our organization is founded, and which, I trust, moves its humblest member. But we have come to sound a warning throughout the length and breadth of the land—a warning which everyone of our own people from Newfoundland to California and from Florida to Alaska must hear and heed. *We are perishing as a people and the land of our fathers shall presently know us no more.* Emerson once said, "What you do speaks so loud I can not hear what you say." Let me here change the words but not the meaning. The facts cry out so loud that we can not hear the vain and wordy opinions of the theorists and the sentimentalists. The prattle of these sentimentalists, be it ever so noisy, can not prevent us from both seeing and hearing the real drama. We are witnessing the greatest tragedy of the ages.

AN INFLUX OF FOREIGNERS

To place these facts in their proper relation, one to another, we must study the map of the United States. That map, hanging on the wall of the old school-house, or facing us over our desks in the library at home, seems always to appear so big and brave and bold. To the child at school it appears to flaunt its very bigness in the face of all the world. My fellow American citizens in all the states, study that map carefully. In terms of the civilization of the whole world it will richly repay investigation. Let us move with the sun from the valley of the river St. Johns in Maine, to the far-off mountains of our California. Incoming masses by the hundred thousand flood New England. They do not speak our language, can not know our laws, and do not mix with our native people because there are hardly any natives in New England left to mix with. In dozens of schools built for the children of the great city of Boston and its suburbs the English language is not even taught, not to speak of as being used as a means of acquiring knowledge or of taking loyal and useful part in our national life. Throughout twenty varieties of the stupendous foreign sections in all our great industrial cities of the North, the very conditions of life prevent millions from learning the English language or tak-

The Ku Klux Kreed

The following creed was presented at the first annual meeting of the Grand Dragons of the Knights of the Ku Klux Klan in Asheville, North Carolina, in July 1923.

We, THE ORDER of the Knights of the Ku Klux Klan, reverentially acknowledge the majesty and supremacy of the Divine Being, and recognize the goodness and providence of the same.

WE RECOGNIZE our relation to the Government of the United States of America, the Supremacy of its Constitution, the Union of States thereunder, and the Constitutional Laws thereof, and we shall be ever devoted to the sublime principles of a pure Americanism and valiant in the defense of its ideals and institutions.

WE AVOW THE distinction between the races of mankind as same has been decreed by the Creator, and shall ever be true in the faithful maintenance of White Supremacy and will strenuously oppose any compromise thereof in any and all things.

WE APPRECIATE the intrinsic value of a real practical fraternal relationship among men of kindred thought, purpose and ideals and the infinite benefits accruable therefrom, and shall faithfully devote ourselves to the practice of an honorable Klanishness that the life and living of each may be a constant blessing to others.

Anti-Movements in America, 1977.

ing an American breath into their nostrils. From St. Louis and Chicago and Milwaukee on the West to New York and Boston on the East democratic American political life is now almost impossible—unthinkable. . . . In our Far Western territory, where a million square miles of mountain and valley are beginning a marvelous development, we Americans are fighting one of the most desperate and crucial social conflicts in the history of our country and of European civilization. Our Western people are striving for the very salvation of our soil as the heritage of the white American. This conflict rages day by day—week by week—year by year. Our brethren of the West are misunderstood and their crying call for help is largely rejected by the East. There are counties in California where more Japanese babies are being born each year than white babies. The Japanese in California are multiplying at the stupendous rate of sixty-nine per thousand, annually, while the white people of California increase at the rate of eighteen per thousand. But the eighteen per cent includes the relatively high rate of the foreign-born whites. The American white people of California increase by an annual rate of less than ten per thousand. Look you well, fellow Americans, to this part of our map. Go on in your indifference and carelessness, and these western valleys and mountains will, in the days of your children, be blood-soaked by one of the most desperate of interracial wars—a war at once civil and international—in the history of the world, and despite all your treaties of peace.

MEXICAN IMMIGRATION

In the Southwest are over eighteen hundred miles of boundary line between ourselves and the people of Mexico. I know that I am expressing for my colleagues of the Ku Klux Klan who dwell along that eighteen hundred miles of boundary line their inmost thought, when I say that they wish only peace and fellowship and mutual aid and generosity to mark all our relations with the simple and kindly people of Mexico. But we are here marshalling the facts—the staggering facts which the American people must know and ponder well today. Nearly half a million Mexicans, speaking various dialects of the Spanish and Indian languages, have recently come across our Southwestern boundary line. Surely it is not with any ill will in our hearts that we say with all the power we have that these thousands can not share our American democracy with us in this generation. In Mexico these people can be ruled in such a way and take such measures of progress as may befit them. Granted time and they may evolve a successful democracy all their own. But in this generation they will make democracy impossible wherever large numbers of them settle among us. If immigration continues through the next generation THEY WILL FOREVER ENCROACH UPON AND OCCUPY OUR SOUTHWEST. The native-born, white American will either become a small ruling class, or fade from sight altogether. There are factories in Texas with practically none but Mexicans employed. There are sections of the Southwest where, in town and on the countryside, there are many Negroes, Mexicans and Japanese, few Americans.

IN THE SOUTH

Finally, we come to the South. . . . We can here take but a rapid glance at the inexorable problem of the Southland. May Providence give to us men and women of the South the power we need to place our problem before our fellow citizens in other sections in such a way as to win their minds and hearts by the goodness of our cause. If I but could, I would move my hand along that ancient and deadly line which separates us from our countrymen and wipe it out forever. Our problem of the Negro, men and women of the North, is your problem. If we fail, you fail. We plead with you to join with us in freeing all our minds from bigotry, all our hearts from unworthy passions, and all our thoughts from sectional misunderstanding.

The larger fact which I seek in this connection to strike into the mind and conscience of my country is as simple as the multiplication-table. The Negro of to-day is less in numbers than the white inhabitants in all states but one, for a single reason. That reason is the high average mortality among the Negroes. The enormous birth rate of the Negro population would rapidly submerge our white population if the Negroes were not decimated by a high death rate. The Negroes' numbers are kept within the number of our white population by various dreadful diseases. Though these diseases afflict us all in the South, the white people are generally far more immune than the blacks. We are somewhat behind the North and West in the practice of medicine, sanitation, and the general prevention of disease. But we are making great strides in this as in other means of progress. As all our people, including the Negroes, are progressively saved from the ravages of disease, the Negroes' birth rate will be more and more relentlessly shown in the census of the living. As night follows day, the Negro will, in the future, move on toward larger and larger comparative numbers in the South.

And so this map of our beloved land, which, as school children, we gazed upon with deep longings toward the future greatness of our country—this map to-day, section by section, is discolored and fading. So do our hopes, too, fade and fail. We Americans are a perishing people, and the things we have inherited and hold dearest in our hearts are on the way to dissolution and total loss. Of all the greater people of history, we Americans least deserve even the pity which is the portion of those who fail. The glory of our rise, the large part that is ours in the present, the majestic hope of the nation which prophesies such a resplendent future—all this is our heritage. We lack only understanding of ourselves and the public spirit required to take action. The Ku Klux Klan, in garb of strange device, marshalled under the flag of our country, has thrust itself as a dire warning across the downward pathway of the American people—our own people, whom we love.

White Supremacy

BISHOP ALMA WHITE

Writing in 1927, Klan supporter Bishop Alma White argues that the supremacy of the white race is revealed in the Bible. According to White, Noah proclaims that his son Ham, the ancestor of the black race, will be the servant of his more successful brother, Japheth, who represents the white race. Those who contradict this divine law by advocating racial equality or racial mixing will face the wrath of God, claims White. Although she strongly advocates racial supremacy, White insists that the Klan is not an enemy of blacks and that the organization intends to serve both the white and the black race. She also contends that the Klan is opposed to violence and that Jews and Catholics have used the media to spread lies about Klan ideals and intentions.

W hite supremacy is an issue of great importance. If some of the colored people are not curbed in their ambition to mix their blood with that of the white race, it will not be long until there will be no such thing as definite racial lines. The Negroes are going north and settling indiscriminately among the whites. Property values are being depreciated by this influx of colored immigration. But little sympathy was shown the South when a race of colored slaves was liberated among them. The North had no conception of what it meant for the white people of the South to preserve the color and racial lines, considering the fact that in some places the population was about equally divided, and there was no cooperation from the North to be had in the struggle. But now, while the problem is still serious in the South, intolerable conditions are developing in some northern localities as the result of this migration of colored people.

Excerpted from *Heroes of the Fiery Cross*, by Bishop Alma White (Zarephath, NJ: Good Citizen, 1928).

After the Civil War, people who came south would persist in their arguments in favor of social equality. They did this chiefly because they had no solution for the racial problems, and nothing could have stirred more effectually the blood of a true Southerner who had the social problem to contend with every day in the year. Invariably, when an advocate of equality was asked if he would be willing for his daughter to marry a black man, his reply would be, "No." Where then was the consistency in his attitude toward the relationship of the races?

Theory is all right in its place, but its practicability is the proof of its merit. There are many dreamers who have advice to give; but let us hear from the people with experience. Perhaps residents in Northern states will be better qualified to formulate theories on a true basis after they have lived in the same locality with Negroes.

WHITE SUPREMACY IN THE BIBLE

The Book of Genesis, in its account of Shem, Ham, and Japheth, sons of Noah, teaches the supremacy of the white race. Ham saw the nakedness of his father, but made no effort to cover him, and a curse was pronounced upon him and his posterity. Noah awoke from his wine and said, "Cursed be Canaan [Ham]; a servant of servants shall he be unto his brethren." "Blessed be the Lord God of Shem; and Canaan shall be his servant." "God shall enlarge Japheth [the white race], and he shall dwell in the tents of Shem; and Canaan shall be his servant" (Gen. 9:25-27). This edict was imposed by a wise and just God, and should not work a hardship on the black race. It cannot be otherwise than that it should be for their good. Until the curse is lifted from the human race, the very best position that the sons of Ham could be placed in is that of servants (not slaves), thus establishing white supremacy as foretold more than four thousand years ago.

At the building of the Tower of Babel God confused the languages to fulfil His purpose in working out the destiny of the races. To break down racial barriers and advocate a mixture of blood would be to subject the world to divine wrath.

The only hope of civilization is to preserve unmixed the blood of the races. "If any man shall add unto these things, God shall add unto him the plagues that are written in this book: and if any man shall take away from the words of the book of this prophecy, God shall take away his part out of the book of life, and out of the holy city, and from the things which are written in this book" (Rev. 22:19).

Presumption leads to ruin and to perdition. Nothing has ever been gained by trying to change the laws of God or the penalties which He has meted out to races and peoples. There must be cooperation with His plans in the administration of justice to all mankind or the penalty will be suffered. When color lines have served their purposes, the Almighty himself will remove the barriers. This will take place some time in the reconstruction period that is coming to the whole world. Then why attempt to force the issue?

THE TRAVESTY OF RACIAL MIXING

It is to be deplored that there are white men of superior intelligence who would take advantage of an inferior race and sell out honor and principle to satisfy their base desires. Such men break the laws of God and man and bring ruin to themselves and their posterity. How great will be their responsibility! Their offspring must bear the stigma of criminal and degraded parentage, whether reared among the blacks or whites. This was a part of the evils of slavery, and present day conditions are as bad, if not worse.

A class of cultured Negroes have organized societies to promote the mixing of white and colored blood. The members of these societies are oath-bound to marry none but white women. This shows the pride of the Negro, who is unwilling to submit to racial bounds and the edicts of Holy Writ. He attempts to take matters in his own hands, but he will only bring calamity upon himself and his race for his presumption. God's laws governing the races are immutable, and woe unto the man who would try to change them.

The Negro's greatest asset is his simplicity of faith in the

New Testament Gospel. When he tries to stretch himself beyond his measure he invariably gets into trouble. The Negro
"spirituals" and the sermons of leading colored evangelists are
everywhere popular and have done much good. In the days of
slavery, many masters on their death-beds preferred to have the
prayers and comfort of some pious slave rather than the services of the parish minister. Let the colored people keep in the

Anglo-Saxon Achievement

*The following passage is excerpted from a paper read at the first
annual meeting of the Grand Dragons of the Knights of the
Ku Klux Klan in Asheville, North Carolina, in July 1923.*

History has no parallel for [our] achievement in government. Klansmen should never forget from what
lands [Washington, Jefferson, and Hamilton] came. And
from what race they sprang. They were North Europeans of the Anglo-Saxon stock, and we of the Anglo-
Saxon blood are proud of the record of our race.

Thus we see, "It is our blood that wrested America
from the wilderness and the savage; won its freedom
and built up its civilization.". . .

In the future as in the past—the hope and destiny of
the nation rests in white supremacy. It will preserve the
doctrines of popular liberty which lie at the foundation
of our government, these ideals which are enshrined in
the constitution of the republic and our free institutions.

And now Klansmen: Of all men we know that only as
we follow in the pathway of the principles of our Anglo-
Saxon fathers and express in our life the spirit and genius
of their ideals may we hope to maintain the supremacy
of the race, and to perpetuate our inheritance of liberty.

Anti-Movements in America, 1977.

place where God appointed them and save themselves from racial suicide and the judgments that would otherwise fall upon them and their posterity.

THE KLAN'S ATTITUDE TOWARD NEGROES

The attitude of the Ku Klux Klan toward the colored people has been grossly and purposely misrepresented by Jews and Roman Catholics, who have used the daily press for their own selfish and political interests. The Negroes have been made to believe that the Klan is their avowed enemy, when nothing could be farther from the truth. All kinds of falsehoods have been propagated about Klan animosity toward them for which there has not been the slightest foundation. Many white people have not understood the source of such fabrications; but one acquainted with the iniquitous system of the Roman-Hebrew alliance needs no enlightenment. This un-American coalition of garbage-can politicians wants the colored man's vote, and it matters little to them how it is gotten.

The Klan is a white, Protestant, Gentile organization whose principles stand as much for the liberty and protection of the colored people as for the white race. It may take years to disillusion them and the general public, where there has been so much misrepresentation, but time will wear down any wall of opposition and bring about the vindication of those who stand for truth and righteousness.

A lie is said to be short-lived, but too often it happens that its destructive work has been accomplished before it can be checked. The colored people have been made to believe that the Klan regalia was designed for the special purpose of intimidating and terrorizing them. Remarks of porters on railroad trains have convinced me of this. On a certain occasion a colored porter, from a Romanized community of Chicago, saw a picture of Klansmen in their robes and remarked, "If I was to see one of them comin' toward me at night I'd kill myse'f runnin'." Another was heard to say, "If ever I gits a letter from the Ku Kluxes I's gonna finish readin' dat letter on de train." And so the contagion has spread until the colored population is thoroughly imbued with the idea that the Klan is secretly watching their activities and planning to do them harm.

OPPOSITION TO VIOLENCE

The Klan is opposed to mob violence and lynchings, and has succeeded in abolishing them in places where they were of frequent occurrence; and yet the patriots are charged with floggings and other cruelties where crimes have been committed by men in disguise. Before the Klan was ever heard of, criminals in disguise were active, both in the North and the South. There was scarcely a daily paper that did not give reports of these night-raiders. There was no one on whom to lay the blame until the Klan arose to safeguard our liberties.

The author could relate a number of instances in connection with her Church where Roman Catholics and Jews resorted to mob violence to keep Christian workers from exercising their constitutional rights in the worship of God. The latter were pelted with eggs and stones and driven from their places of worship by these men in disguise, aided by Roman Catholic police. One such occasion was at Plainfield, New Jersey, in 1915, where the offenders brandished revolvers in the faces of Protestant ministers and others, boarded trolley cars and trains and followed them for miles out of the city, after the police, standing in the shadows, had superintended the cutting down of the tent. Now from the same political sources comes the wholesale denunciation of the Knights of the Ku Klux Klan, laying to their charge acts of violence to prejudice the public mind. Governor Alfred E. Smith, the outstanding candidate for the presidential nomination by the Democratic Party, made known his opinion of the Klan in a letter dated December 29, 1927, to the Klan representative of Queen's County, Long Island. Governor Smith is quoted in the New York *World* of December 30 as saying: "I regard the purposes of your organization with abhorrence and I consider them subversive of the fundamentals of American democracy." Read the principles of the Klan . . . and consider whether you want a man elected president who abhors them.

The Decline
of the 1920s' Klan

MILTON MELTZER

The Ku Klux Klan reached the peak of its power in the mid-1920s,
notes Milton Meltzer in the following selection. The organization
became so influential that it was able to affect many local and state
elections, and several Klansmen or Klan supporters were elected as
sheriffs, superintendents, senators, and governors. Meltzer surmises
that the Klan's appeal to religious prejudice was partly responsible
for the defeat of Alfred Smith, a Catholic Democrat, in the presidential election of 1928. The early twentieth century Klan quickly
declined, however, when news about Klan violence and political
scandals involving Klan leadership became public. Meltzer is the author of *The Truth About the Ku Klux Klan*.

B y 1925 the Klan was Big Business. Almost six million
Americans belonged to it during the Twenties, and they
paid $75 million a year into its treasury. That August, caravans
of cars and dozens of chartered trains bearing Kluxers from
around the nation poured into the city of Washington with
KKK signs chalked on their sides. On Saturday afternoon, August 8, forty thousand hooded Klansmen and women paraded
down Pennsylvania Avenue to the Washington Monument.
Their marching bands blared "Onward Christian Soldiers" and
as the crowds lining the sidewalks cheered, the Kluxers raised
their right arms in salute.

THE PEAK OF KLAN POWER

The peak of Klan power came during the 1920s. So strong had
the Klan become that in Oregon it was able to elect the Presi-

dent of the State Senate and the Speaker of the House. In Ohio, where perhaps 400,000 joined the Invisible Empire, Klan-supported candidates became mayors of Toledo, Akron, and Columbus. In Texas, 200,000 joined, and Earl Mayfield was the first Klansman to be elected to the U.S. Senate. In Waco the Mayor and Board of Police Commissioners were Klansmen. So were scores and scores of sheriffs throughout the state. In California the Klan captured the state legislature with its candidates.

In an Arkansas election the Klan swept almost every office in Little Rock. The Klan was so entrenched in Alabama that it could elect Klansmen Bibb Graves and Charles McCall governor and attorney general. Klan candidates were elected mayor of Emporia and to other local offices in Kansas.

William Allen White, editor of the Emporia *Gazette,* urged all citizens to oppose the Klan:

> The Ku Klux Klan is an organization of cowards. Not a man in it has the courage of his convictions. It is an organization of traitors to American institutions. Not a man in it has faith enough in American courts, laws and officials, to trust them to maintain law and order. . . . It is a menace to peace and decent neighborly living. . . . For a self-constituted body of moral idiots who would substitute the findings of the Ku Klux Klan for the processes of law, to try to better conditions, would be a most un-American outrage which every good citizen should resent.

> It is a national menace, this Klan. It knows no party. It knows no country. It knows only bigotry, malice and terror. Our national government is founded upon reason, and the Golden Rule. This Klan is preaching terror and force.

The Klan won so many followers in Indiana that in 1923 it could assemble 100,000 of them in a field near Kokomo to crown David Stephenson the Grand Dragon of the Realm of Indiana. "He sold fright," said a reporter, "as he had sold coal, in carload lots." He paraded legions of his hooded knights through black and Catholic districts of the cities. Enrolling 240,000 members in the state, he elected two senators, two governors and the legislature. For a while he made the state an appendage to the Klan.

New York put 200,000 Klansmen on the rolls and Pennsylvania 225,000. In the New England states, Connecticut provided 20,000 and Maine 15,000.

Except for Indiana, the Klan did best in the state of Colorado. It began its work in Denver in 1921 and in scarcely three years converted the state into one of its strongest realms. Enlisting 35,000 members, the Klan became the dominant power in state and local politics. Under Grand Dragon John G. Locke, it took over the Republican Party and in the 1924 election won control of Colorado. The Klan elected a U.S. Senator, the governor, lieutenant-governor, secretary of state, attorney general, superintendent of public instruction, and a state supreme court justice. Skillful political organizing methods at the grass roots level did it. Once in office, the Klan governor filled every position he could with Klansmen.

THE KLAN AND PRESIDENTIAL ELECTIONS

The presidential election of 1924 gave the Klan a chance to show its national strength. At the Democratic Convention in New York it is estimated that at least 350 delegates—over one-fourth of the total number—were Klansmen. They were responsible for defeating an anti-Klan plank in the platform and for the failure of Governor Alfred Smith, a Catholic, to win the party's nomination.

The Republicans offered little better. Their candidate, President Calvin Coolidge, believed the White House should do nothing about lynching, disfranchisement, or discrimination in federal employment. When some delegates proposed an anti-Klan plank at the Republican Convention, the leadership had it quietly buried in committee.

The next presidential contest, in 1928, stood out because of a carefully orchestrated whispering campaign that played on religious prejudice. This time Alfred Smith had won the Democratic nomination. The Republicans spread it about that if he entered the White House the Pope would come to Washington to run the country. The Klan preferred the Republican candidate, Herbert Hoover. Although he was a Quaker, that was some sort of Protestant. Again the Klan scattered nation-

Klan Violence

Reports about threats and physical attacks perpetuated by the Klan appeared in newspapers in the 1920s.

From late 1920 through 1921, local Klaverns' violence and vigilante tactics began hitting the newspapers. On the eve of the 1920 election, when Warren Harding won the presidency, large numbers of Klansmen paraded through Southwestern towns, warning blacks to stay away from the polls. The smaller encounters were worse. In Houston a prosperous black dentist was "irreparably mutilated" by a gang of disguised Klansmen who claimed he had been consorting with a white woman. In Bolton, Texas, a black youth who had been jailed for "insulting a white woman" was kidnapped from jail and severely beaten; a placard attached to his back said, *Whipped by the K.K.K.* In Miami, an archdeacon of the Episcopal church was stripped and whipped by eight Klansmen who condemned him for preaching "racial equality." In Birmingham, the white proprietor of a butcher shop was flogged for his "friendly relations" with blacks. In Pensacola, Florida, a Klansman drove up to a Greek restaurateur and handed him a note reading, "You are an undesirable citizen. You violate the Federal Prohibition Laws and laws of decency and are a running sore on society. Several trains are leaving Pensacola daily. Take your choice, but do not take too much time. Sincerely in earnest, K.K.K."

Wyn Craig Wade, *The Fiery Cross: The Ku Klux Klan in America*, 1987.

wide copies of its phony "Knights of Columbus Oath." Scary headlines in its press read: ROMAN CATHOLIC CLERICAL PARTY OPENS BIG DRIVE TO CAPTURE AMERICA FOR THE POPE. Smith's supporters confronted the issue, called the election a battle between Smith and the Klan. But 1928 was not a Democratic year, and Hoover won.

What the election showed was that America was not immune to intolerance. The appeal to racial and religious prejudice that Hitler was making in Germany in those years found response among millions here, too.

THE KLAN'S DISINTEGRATION

Taking power proved easier for the Klan than using it. Colorado's Klan administration failed to produce results to please anyone and, after one term in office, was defeated. Nationwide, the Klan crumbled and disintegrated by the end of the Twenties. When Klansmen gained office, hostile legislators and bureaucrats often managed to block them. As the movement lost its political influence, its followers dropped away.

Scandals, too, did much to bleed the Klan. As early as 1921 a Congressional investigation exposed Klan racketeering. Even while the Klan rode high in Colorado, for instance, its violence and corruption came to light and decline set in. David Stephenson, Indiana's Klan leader, was convicted of raping and murdering a young woman and sent to prison for life.

National and state Klan leaders struggled for control, and in their attempts to unseat one another, exposed how they abused the powers of their offices and violated the Klan's proclaimed principles of moral decency. Internal quarrels disheartened the membership and weakened the Klan's reputation and power. When driven out of office, some leaders formed Klan-like rival organizations and then became ensnared in costly lawsuits that did the Klan still more damage. Many Klan groups gave up and disbanded. Members who thought they had joined to fight for morality found too much immorality within their own ranks. The Klan's pure white robes had become stained and dishonored.

Why did the Klan fail after reaching so much power? Sociologists studying the life of such movements have offered some answers. They think that the Klan of the Twenties never had inspiring leaders or any great unifying ideals. It was planless and opportunistic. Its program was defensive. It preached action against evils which were often more imaginary than real. Like its ancestor of Reconstruction days, it was loosely organized with no central commanding authority. Like that first Klan, it was also anti-democratic, violent, uncontrollable. Historian David Chalmers concludes: "The failure of the Ku Klux Klan to anchor itself as a successful feature in American life was due more to its own ineptness than any other cause or combination of factors. The decline of the Klan as a mass movement in America was its own fault, nobody else's."

Which leads one to ask: suppose its terror had not gone so far, its leaders had not been so inept, its program not so negative? What would have happened to America?

CHAPTER 3

WHITE
SEPARATIST
MOVEMENTS
OF THE
MID–TWENTIETH
CENTURY

AMERICAN
SOCIAL
MOVEMENTS

One Klan Dies, Another Rises: The New Klan

RICHARD K. TUCKER

Several new Klan groups emerged after the U.S. Supreme Court's 1954 ruling against racial segregation in public schools, writes Richard K. Tucker in the following selection. As more civil rights laws were passed in the 1960s—upsetting those with segregationist sentiments—the Klan became increasingly violent. Klansmen and Klan allies murdered civil rights workers and bombed buses and churches, yet the men convicted of these crimes received relatively light sentences, Tucker notes. Klan membership dropped dramatically by the 1980s, however, with a growing public contempt of racially motivated violence and with stronger legal actions against white supremacist extremists. Tucker is the author of *The Dragon and the Cross: The Rise and Fall of the Ku Klux Klan in Middle America.*

[A fter the 1920s] the Invisible Empire never recovered in Middle America. Vestiges remained. But the David Curtis Stephenson scandal [Stephenson, an Indiana Klan leader, was convicted of rape and murder in 1928] and the exposés of Klan political corruption spread like a plague from Indiana east, west, and north, across the realms where the now-disgraced Grand Dragon had once been a charismatic organizer and a symbol of patriotism and Christian virtue.

Whatever was left of the empire was seldom invisible. As public concern grew over the invasion of political processes by a secret society, state after state had passed antimask laws.

Excerpted from *The Dragon and the Cross: The Rise and Fall of the Ku Klux Klan in Middle America,* by Richard K. Tucker (North Haven, CT: Archon Books, 1991). Copyright © 1991 by Richard K. Tucker. Reprinted by permission of the publisher.

Klansmen could still parade if they wanted to, but no longer with hoods to hide their faces.

In the South strong roots remained, but violence by Klan extremists against both blacks and whites had turned increasing numbers of people against the entire movement. Nationally, internal dissensions and power struggles had taken their toll. At the same time, the public emotions that had fueled the Klan—the flag-waving frenzy left over from World War I, reaction against Jazz Age morality and the Demon Rum, fear that the Pope of Rome was about to take over America—were subsiding. The Klan had provided an outlet for these tensions, and now the pressure was running low. . . .

Enough of the Klan antipapist spirit survived to be a major factor in the defeat of Catholic Al Smith in his 1928 bid for the presidency. But by 1930, the national membership of more than five million once claimed by the Invisible Empire had dropped to under 300,000, mostly in the South.

Then, as the Depression spread across the land, what remained of the Klan offered no solutions or hope for the growing millions of unemployed. Even if it had, few could spare the ten-dollar initiation fee, plus six to seven dollars for a robe. By the 1940s, America was again at war. The Pope as the nation's perceived enemy was largely forgotten as Americans united against more real enemies—the warlords of Japan and the Nazi barbarians of Germany.

PERSISTING RACISM

Still, Klan or no Klan, strong currents of racism persisted in American life. In 1943, in the midst of the war effort, race riots erupted in Detroit, where new waves of blacks and whites from the South had come to work in war industries. Thirty-four people were killed and hundreds injured before troops came in to quell the disorders.

Racism continued in the military. Black and white troops were still segregated, and blacks were routinely relegated to menial jobs. Black officers could not enter white officers' clubs. In England there were even lynchings of black soldiers by their white fellow Americans because the blacks had dated white English girls.

It was this same racism that, in the 1950s and 1960s, brought forth a new Ku Klux Klan in the South from its Reconstruction, white supremacist origins. It was smaller but more violent than any of its predecessors. This new one-track, paranoid-racist Klan became the terrorist guerrilla wing of the South's massive resistance to a new age of civil rights for blacks.

NEW KLAN GROUPS

As early as 1953, a new, small Klan group called, redundantly, the U.S. Klans, Knights of the Ku Klux Klan, had been formed in Atlanta by an auto plant worker named Eldon Edwards. He had little success until about two years later, after a U.S. Supreme Court decision and follow-up court mandate had sent shock waves through the white supremacist South.

The first alarm sounded on May 17, 1954, when the court outlawed racial segregation in public schools. (Ironically, the decision came not on a case from the Deep South, but from Topeka, Kansas, which had long maintained separate elementary schools for blacks and whites.) The aftershock came in 1955 when the court mandated that racial desegregation of public schools proceed "with all deliberate speed."

With these threats to white supremacy growing, in September 1956 Edwards attracted some three thousand to a Klan rally on Stone Mountain, near Atlanta, where Colonel Simmons had started his Invisible Empire more than forty years earlier. Within two years, an estimated fifteen thousand had joined his new Klan.

Edwards died in 1960, but more powerful leaders took over. One of the largest of the new groups was the United Klans of America, organized by Robert Shelton, an Alabama salesman. The United Klans soon became a sort of loosely knit empire across the South. By 1965, Klan membership had grown to between thirty-five and fifty thousand.

Southern political leaders, while not openly endorsing the Klan, helped create the climate for its growth. On January 19,

1956, the Alabama State Legislature passed a "nullification" resolution, asserting a state's right to negate Supreme Court rulings in its jurisdiction. On February 21 of the same year—again hearkening back more than a century and a half to the "interposition" and "nullification" resolutions drafted by Thomas Jefferson and James Madison against the Alien and Sedition acts—the Virginia State Legislature passed another "interposition resolution," claiming a state's right to interpose its sovereignty against enactments or rulings from the federal government.

Both turned out to be empty political gestures. But in March 1956, a call by 101 southern congressmen for "massive resistance" to the school desegregation order "by all lawful means" inspired a broader audience. Southern politicians began wearing "Never!" (to school integration) labels on their coat lapels. "White Citizens Councils" began organizing to put economic and social pressures on any supporters of, or even moderates on, new civil rights for blacks.

THE ADVENT OF CIVIL RIGHTS

The school integration battles were only part of the picture. As new civil rights laws and court rulings came from Washington, D.C., the South felt increasingly besieged. In 1956, the Supreme Court banned racially segregated seating on city buses in Birmingham, Alabama, after a year-long boycott by blacks brought a test case. In 1960, in a case from Virginia, the Supreme Court outlawed racial segregation in interstate bus terminals. In 1964, in a sweeping "omnibus" Civil Rights Act, Congress outlawed racial discrimination in a broad spectrum of American life—public accommodations, housing, jobs, and public services. In 1965, a new Voting Rights Act, strongly promoted by President Lyndon Johnson, authorized federal officials to supervise voter registration in states where blacks had been systematically blocked from the registration rolls.

The South fought back on legal grounds but repeatedly lost. Resistance to race mixing by lawful means was clearly not working, and nowhere was this fact more challenging than in the minds of the new Klan. In such a climate the new Klan grew and its violence escalated. From 1956 to 1966, there were more than one thousand documented cases of racist terrorism, assaults, and murders committed by Klansmen and their allies. The victims were both black and white.

KLAN VIOLENCE

In May 1961, in Anniston, Alabama, Klansmen led a white gang that firebombed the first Freedom Riders bus, where blacks and whites had joined to test the new bus terminal desegregation ruling, and later beat them when they arrived on a second bus in Birmingham. The nation was shocked when, in September 1963, four young black girls were killed in a bomb explosion in their church in Birmingham. The girls, one eleven and three fourteen, were in a room adjoining an outside wall where Klansmen had planted a dynamite bomb. Shortly after the bombing, a white supremacist was quoted as telling a group of Klansmen that the men who planted the bomb deserved medals. The girls in the church, he said, were "just little niggers . . . and if there's four less niggers tonight, then I say, 'good for whoever planted the bomb.'"

Despite new federal laws, killing was still a state crime to be prosecuted in state courts. In case after case, accused Klan or allied racist killers went free in trials before all-white southern juries. Tom Coleman, a part-time deputy sheriff who admitted shooting Jonathan Daniels, a white civil rights worker in Fort Deposit, Alabama, in 1965, was indicted for manslaughter, but it took an all-white jury only two hours to acquit him.

Two Klansmen who shot and killed Lieutenant Colonel Lemuel Penn, a black army reserve officer, as he drove through Georgia on his return trip to Washington, D.C., were identified by the driver of the Klan car from which they fired. They were charged with the killing, but they were also acquitted by another all-white jury.

Other cases never even came to trial. The F.B.I. investigated the dynamite bombing of the Birmingham church where the four young black girls were killed. An eyewitness told them he had seen Klansmen plant the bomb. Still, no one was charged. It was fourteen years later before the case was reopened by Alabama attorney-general William Baxley. By then the social and legal climate had changed somewhat. A seventy-nine-year-old Klansman named Robert Chambliss was charged with first-degree murder in the bombing, found guilty by a jury, and sentenced to life. More than one Klansman had obviously been involved, but no one else was ever charged in the bombing case.

The disappearance of three civil rights workers in Mississippi in 1964 attracted national attention. An investigation by the F.B.I., along with federal reward money, finally produced information that their bodies were buried in an earthen dam near Philadelphia, Mississippi. Michael Schwerner and Andrew Goodman, both white and from New York, and James Chaney, who was black, had, as later revealed, been shot to death by Klansmen with the connivance of a deputy sheriff.

Still, no state murder charges were brought. It was only when the U.S. Justice Department called a federal grand jury into the case that indictments charging civil rights violations were secured against nineteen men, including Klansmen and their deputy sheriff accomplice. Seven were convicted in the killings, but only on federal civil rights violations. The murders were proved, but the maximum sentence any of the accused could, and did, receive under the federal law was ten years in prison for "conspiracy to violate civil rights."

Viola Liuzzo

The case of Viola Liuzzo in Alabama in 1965 was even more illustrative of the reluctance of the besieged white supremacist South to deal with Klan racist killers. Mrs. Liuzzo, a thirty-nine-year-old white housewife and mother from Detroit, had gone to Alabama in March 1965 to help blacks in their second march from Selma. She had volunteered to shuttle loads of blacks in her car for the march. On the night of March 25, she was driving back to Montgomery to pick up more black marchers, accompanied by a young black man, Leroy Moton.

On a desolate stretch of road in Lowndes County, her car was pursued and overtaken by a carload of Klansmen. As the Klan car pulled alongside, Mrs. Liuzzo looked to see who had been following her. From the back seat of the Klan car a man fired two shots from a .38 caliber pistol, killing Mrs. Liuzzo instantly. Moton escaped further harm by feigning death.

Three Klansmen—Eugene Thomas, William Orville Eaton, and Collie Leroy Wilkins—were indicted for the murder. The state's case against them was strong. Moton described how they had been pursued. More important, one passenger in the Klan car was an undercover F.B.I. agent who said he had seen Wilkins fire the fatal shots.

In Wilkins's murder trial in May 1965, his defense attorney, Klan "Imperial Klonsel" Matt Murphy, Jr., brought forth no witness to discredit the eyewitness testimony. Instead, in his summation to the jury, he delivered a long, antiblack, anti-Semitic, anti-Communist harangue that exploited the depths of southern redneck racism:

> And this white woman who got killed? White woman? Where's that NAACP card? I thought I'd never see the day when Communists and niggers and white niggers and Jews were flying under the banner of the United Nations flag, not the American flag we fought for.
>
> I'm proud to be a white man and I'm proud that I stand up on my feet for white supremacy. Not black supremacy, not the mixing and mongrelization of the races . . . not the Zionists that run that bunch of niggers. The white people are not gonna run before them. And when white people join up to 'em them become white niggers.
>
> Do you know those big black niggers were driven by the woman, sitting right in the back seat? Niggers! One white woman and these niggers. Right there. Riding right through your county. Communists dominate them niggers.
>
> You know what that nigger [Moton] said on the stand. No. Yeah. No. Yeah. Like a 10-year-old boy. He should have

been saying Yes, Sir, and No, Sir before that honorable white judge. But the buck hasn't got the sense, the morals, or the decency.

I said now look, boy. Look down at your feets. Niggers only understand this kind of talk. How many feets away was that car? So he looked down at his feet and said about 25 feet away. . . . He said he passed out for 25–30 minutes. . . . What's he doing down there all that time? In that car *alone* with that woman.

Then the nigger ran up the road and a truck came by and he stopped it. There was a rabbi in that truck. A rabbi. Of course he stopped and put the nigger in the back. And there they were—rabbi with a nigger . . . white woman, nigger man, nigger woman—all in there, feet to feet.

Integration breaks every moral law God ever wrote. Noah's son was Ham and committed adultery and was banished and his sons were Hamites and God banished them and they went to Africa and the only thing they ever built was grass huts. No white woman can ever marry a descendant of Ham. That's God's law. . . . I don't care what Lyndon Johnson or anybody else says.

After ten hours deliberation, the jury announced that it was hopelessly deadlocked. A retrial was ordered. In the second trial in October 1965, it took another white jury only two hours to find Wilkins and his fellow Klansmen not guilty of either murder or conspiracy.

Again, the federal government moved in. Wilkins, Thomas, and Eaton were indicted and tried on federal charges of conspiring to violate civil rights. They were found guilty and sentenced to ten years in prison for a crime that in other areas could have brought Wilkins the death penalty.

A Doomed War

Violent and determined as it seemed, the new southern Klan's guerrilla war—along with the rest of the South's "massive resistance"—against new equality for blacks was doomed from the start. It is more than a cliché to say that civil rights for American blacks was a long-delayed idea whose time had come. By the 1980s, blacks and whites would be sharing school-rooms, bus seats, hotels, and restaurants on an equal basis, in both North and South. By federal law, banks would have signs at their counters advising customers not only that they could not discriminate on the basis of race, religion, or national origin, but also that they could appeal if they believed their rights had been violated. Companies advertising for help would proclaim that they were equal opportunity employers, even if they didn't always follow through. Black men would become mayors of major cities: Atlanta, Baltimore, New York, and, in one less fortunate case, Washington, D.C. In Virginia in 1989, a grandson of black slaves, L. Douglas Wilder, became governor.

Still, laws and political victories could not erase the persisting currents of racism in American life. Millions of whites, in both North and South, while accepting the idea of equal rights for blacks, were still not ready to accept them as social equals. Despite equal opportunity employers, blacks complained they were often the last to be hired and first to be fired. Racism itself, however, had gone underground. In public life, in mainline politics, in business and advertising, it had become a sensitive area to be avoided at all costs.

When David Duke, a racist and former Klansman, won a Republican seat in the Louisiana State Legislature in 1988, mainline Republican leaders rushed to disavow both him and the Klan. When he sought the Republican nomination for the U.S. Senate in the 1990 Louisiana primary election, Republican leaders again disavowed him and supported his Democratic opponent. Duke lost, but, campaigning in a lower key, calling for reforms in the affirmative action program and more equality of opportunity for whites, he managed to get 44 percent of the total vote and 60 percent of the white vote. . . .

Meanwhile, estimated total Klan membership, which had climbed to forty-two thousand at the height of the civil rights battles in 1965, had dropped to about fifteen hundred in 1974.

By 1981 it rose again to an estimated eleven thousand, but by 1988 it had dropped again to about five thousand.

The ups and downs seemed to coincide with changes in the American social and legal climate. The first dramatic drop came after the Klan had clearly lost its battle to stop racial integration in the late 1960s and early 1970s. The resurgence was at least in part a rally on new fronts with broader targets: affirmative action for blacks, Vietnamese fishermen, gay rights, "Jewish conspiracies.". . .

The drop-off of nearly 50 percent by 1988 coincided with a growing public revulsion against Klan bigotry and violence and the better police work and stronger legal action that followed. Between 1979 and 1985, the U.S. Justice Department prosecuted at least eighty-four Klansmen for racially motivated violence. At the state level, juries were no longer reluctant to convict Klan members for criminal acts.

In addition, entire Klan organizations were being held legally responsible for the acts of their members. Klansmen had been convicted on criminal charges for the 1981 lynching of a black youth—Michael Donald—in Mobile, Alabama. But in a civil suit that followed—brought by the Southern Poverty Law Center of Montgomery, Alabama—their parent group, the United Klans of America, was ordered in 1987 to pay seven million dollars in damages to Michael Donald's mother. The United Klans didn't have such money, of course, but continued seizure of their assets put serious restrictions on their activities. Despite anonymous threats on his life, Morris Dees, the courageous attorney of the law center's Klanwatch project continued to fight organizers and inciters of racist violence. They suffered an even heavier blow in 1990 for their alleged responsibility in the killing of Mulugeta Seraw, an Ethiopian student beaten to death by Skinheads in Portland, Oregon, in 1988. The convicted Skinheads—members of one of several gangs of disaffected youth being recruited in northern cities by white-supremacist extremists—said they had been organized and encouraged by agents of the White Aryan Resistance and two of its leaders, Tom and John Metzger.

In a subsequent damage suit brought by the Southern Poverty Law Center and the Anti-Defamation League of B'nai B'rith, the Metzgers, their Aryan Resistance group, and two Skinheads were ordered to pay twelve and one half million dollars in damages to Seraw's family. They had not even a fraction of this amount, but seizure of their available assets was expected to continue.

BRANCHES OF THE KLAN

Names of the continuing Klan groups varied. The United Klans of America continued as a sort of umbrella group for several other units. But, increasingly, the Klan became a magnet for violent affiliated racist groups spreading into the North and Northwest. Aryan Nations, White Aryan Resistance, The Order, The Brotherhood, Skinheads. Whatever their names or organizational structures, however, they were inevitably fixed in the public mind as branches of the Ku Klux Klan, whose name itself had become anathema, even among Americans who shared many of its racial prejudices. Few Americans could be expected to join or support a Klan whose members were known to have infiltrated military posts in North Carolina—the Marine base at Camp LeJeune and army installations at Fort Bragg—to steal rifles, ammunition, and grenades—apparently for a coming race war, or perhaps a revolution against ZOG—the Zionist Occupational Government—in Washington, D.C. In other areas, members of Klan-leaning, neo-Nazi groups like Aryan Nations or The Order had been arrested and convicted of armed robberies to finance their cause.

The "100 percent American" Klan that had once rallied Middle America in defense of flag and Christian virtue was long gone. It had been split by the ambitions and infighting of its leaders, shattered in 1925 by the greed and lusts of an oversexed Grand Dragon, and finally swallowed up in the Great Depression and World War II. What remained of the Klan in the 1990s had become only the nucleus of a paranoid fringe of American society, self-destructing through the crime and violence of its own rank-and-file.

The Citizens' Councils of America

JOHN GEORGE AND LAIRD WILCOX

John George and Laird Wilcox discuss the southern community groups—known as Citizens' Councils—that sprang up after the 1954 Supreme Court ruling that outlawed racial segregation in schools. The Councils opposed racial integration as un-Christian and un-American, yet distinguished themselves from the more combative Klan, emphasizing that their members were law-abiding, respectable citizens. A Citizens' Council periodical, *The Councilor*, influenced white segregationist thought in the 1960s and 1970s. George and Wilcox are the authors of *Nazis, Communists, Klansmen, and Others on the Fringe*, from which this selection is excerpted.

O n May 17, 1954, the United States Supreme Court issued its famous *Brown vs. Board of Education* ruling, which effectively outlawed racially "separate but equal" school systems. Predictably, this sparked a massive revolt among white segregationists, primarily in the Deep South, and led to the formation of a movement (to resist integration) known as the "Citizens' Councils." According to George Thayer in *The Farther Shores of Politics*:

> Within two months of "The Decision," as it came to be known in the South, the First Council was organized in Indianola, Mississippi. It was the first of hundreds of Citizens' Councils to spring up throughout Dixie during the next twelve months.

> Hard-core members of a local Council varied in number from ten or so up to two dozen; nearly all of them repre-

sented the more prosperous segments of the community: businessmen, lawyers, planters, political officials. The structure of each council was uncomplicated and flexible, free of Klan jargon and fancy titles.[1]

They usually did not refer to themselves as "White Citizens Councils," but several unaffiliated groups bore that name. An attempt to discuss their ideology as a whole would be useless, since this varied to a significant extent from council to council. The common characteristic was, of course, opposition to racial integration—they usually labeled their position "segregationist."

THE "UPTOWN KLAN"

Interestingly, it was the development of the Citizens' Councils that may have been partially responsible for the relative weakness of the Ku Klux Klan in the 1960s. Seymour Martin Lipset and Earl Raab have explained:

> The "respectable" southerners who resisted integration sought to emphasize that they were law-abiding. They stressed their differences with the more militant Klan. Their concern with respectability was almost obsessive. Their propaganda stressed that their leadership is drawn from among the "best people," that they include "the most prominent, well-educated and conservative businessmen in each community."[2]

A similar characteristic of the councils appears in Francis M. Wilhoit's *The Politics of Massive Resistance:*

> Though the Councils have been linked with the Klan through such epithets as "white-collar Klan," "uptown Klan," "button-down Klan," and "country club Klan," they usually disdained the cruder forms of lawlessness perpetrated by the Klan and preferred subtler forms of resistance. They have refused to open their membership records to scholarly researchers, but the best estimate is that in their heyday, around 1957, the Councils had about 250,000 members. In-

cluded among their members were bankers, industrialists, lawyers, doctors, judges, congressmen, and governors. And because of their prestigious membership rosters, they had a good deal more success than the Klan in achieving respectability and in politicizing the segregationist masses.[3]

In drawing from the potential Ku Klux Klan membership pool the Citizens' Councils also produced an unfortunate effect: they insured that the Klan wound up with a membership less respectable and less restrained in observing legal amenities than it otherwise might have had. Unlike the "second" Klan of the 1920s, which was more-or-less family- and community-oriented, the "third" Klan of the 1960s had more than a fair share of riff-raff, which may have added somewhat to the level of Klan violence. Unlike the Klan, which was heavily infiltrated by the FBI between 1964 and 1971, the Citizens' Councils were virtually ignored.[4]

One group, the Citizens Council of Greater New Orleans, issued pamphlets against buying records by Negro artists because "rhythm and blues" was considered a corrupting influence on youth. Another of its pamphlets urged southerners, "Don't ever buy a Ford again!" The profits of Ford, the group charged, were being used to push integration. (These tactics, which seem backward and repressive when we associate them with racism, are still used today by groups attempting to boycott rock music or blacklist firms for doing business with South Africa, publishing "pornography," or because of environmental transgressions.)

THE COUNCIL PHILOSOPHY

An early Citizens' Council pamphlet gave an ominous hint at their philosophy:

> The Citizens' Council is the South's answer to the mongrelizers. We will not be integrated! We are proud of our white blood and our white heritage of six centuries. . . . If we are bigoted, prejudiced, un-American, etc., so were George Washington, Thomas Jefferson, Abraham Lincoln,

and other illustrious forebears who believed in segregation. We choose the old pathos of our founding fathers and refuse to appease anyone, even the internationalists.[5]

When the movement was just starting, a list of its recommended literature included Gerald L.K. Smith's anti-Semitic *The Cross and the Flag.* This list was later suppressed to a great extent when many councils tried to woo Jews, especially rabbis. One early pamphlet entitled "A Jewish View of Segregation" attempted to show that southern Jews were segregationists. Most council leaders were careful to avoid overt anti-Semitism, and this was especially true of the largest council organization, Citizens' Councils of America [CCA], headquartered in Jackson, Mississippi, whose publication, *The Citizen,* was edited by W.J. Simmons.

In an early Citizens' Council pamphlet decrying the 1954 Supreme Court decision, Tom Brady, a Mississippi circuit court judge, noted:

> It is lamentable that attention should be called to the alarming increase of Jewish names in the ranks of Communist-front organizations of this country. . . . There are those today who would damn the Jew, who would like to see him persecuted because he controls the motion picture industry, the clothing industry, the jewelry market, and so on. His excellence in these and numerous fields of business endeavor is the result of his own inherent intelligence and industry.[6]

Founded in 1956 in New Orleans, the first convention of the CCA entertained delegates from local Citizens' Councils from Alabama, Arkansas, Florida, Georgia, Louisiana, Mississippi, Tennessee, Texas, Virginia, and the Carolinas. Robert B. Patterson, founder of the Indianola Citizens' Council, was appointed executive secretary. Roy V. Harris, a Georgia state representative for over twenty years and later a member of the Georgia Board of Regents, became chairman. Harris was also publisher of the weekly *Augusta Courier,* founded in 1946, which claimed a national readership in 1967 of ten thousand.

The paper carried articles about alleged black inferiority and the benefits of segregation.

In the early 1960s there were some five hundred local councils and *The Citizen* had a circulation of 34,000. Articles appeared by far-right illuminaries such as Governor George Wallace (Alabama), Major General Edwin A. Walker, Governor Ross R. Barnett (Mississippi), newspaper columnist James J. Kilpatrick, and Medford Evans, managing editor of *The Citizen* as well as a contributing editor of the John Birch Society monthly magazine, *American Opinion*. A weekly radio broadcast was carried on approximately 450 stations.

The Citizen viewed racial segregation as entirely consistent with Christian principles and integration as un-American. An article in 1973 by Rev. G.T. Gillespie noted:

> While the Bible contains no clear mandate for or against segregation between the white and negro races, it does furnish considerable data from which valid inferences may be drawn in support of the general principles of segregation as an important feature of the Divine purpose and Providence throughout the ages.[7]

TRANSIENT MEMBERSHIP

An interesting aspect of the Citizens' Councils (and of right-wing extremist groups generally) is the transient nature of membership. According to Thayer:

> The size of the Citizens' Councils has always been a subject of speculation. Current estimates (1967) put the membership near the 300,000 mark, with 80,000 in Mississippi alone. (Roy) Harris, for one, says the Councils grow and die over a short span of time. "When Martin Luther King comes to Georgia," he said, "there are Citizens' Councils all over the place; when he's not around you can't even get a meeting."[8]

We feel that Wilhoit's figure of 250,000 is closer to the mark, or perhaps even a little high, but a report by Milton Ellerin of the American Jewish Committee estimated a combined Citizens' Councils membership of around *one million* before the 1964 election campaign.[9]

Inflated estimates of the strength of extremist groups do little to enhance our capacity to deal with them, and may tend to encourage repressive abuses. Moreover, even a reliable membership figure may say very little about the actual strength of an organization. A large number of mere card-carriers may be far less significant than a very small disciplined cadre organized as an affinity group. In the case of the Citizens' Councils, the vast majority of members were mere card-carriers whose interest in the organization was fleeting.

COUNCIL TACTICS

Like extremist groups today, the Citizens' Councils engaged in a variety of tactics to force their views on others. One of these was the economic boycott. George Thayer has written:

> The Councils' power was such that it was able to bring the Falstaff Brewing Company to its knees. A story, published in John Hamilton's *White Sentinel* in the fall of 1955, stated that the brewing company had bought a life membership in the NAACP for one of its salesmen. The article went on to suggest that those who disagreed with such activities should refrain from drinking that brand of beer. Sales must have slipped considerably in the South, for in no time at all a Falstaff vice-president was on his way to talk things over with the Council. To the immense satisfaction of Council officials, the Falstaff Brewing Company released a statement disavowing any support for the NAACP: thus the boycott, if there ever was one, was called off.[10]

The Citizens' Councils in Virginia were particularly strident and dogmatic. Headed by John Kasper of the Seaboard Citizens' Council, who wrote in his pamphlet, *Virginians On Guard:* "Hang the nine Supreme Court swine; destroy all Red, Rooseveltian dupes, and death to usurers," they urged all southerners to defy the federal government and demanded that local authorities arrest any federal judge or FBI agent who meddled in their local affairs.[11]

THE COUNCILOR

Perhaps the most influential in the Citizens' Council orbit was a publication of the Citizens' Council of Louisiana, Inc., called *The Councilor*, which billed itself as "A Responsible Voice From Middle-Class America." Founded in 1962, this twelve-to sixteen-page bimonthly was the creation of Ned Touchstone, an open racist who urged white women never to shop alone "in any city with more than 15 percent negro population because civil rights organizations are urging young negro males to 'attack, attack, attack.'"[12]

According to the Anti-Defamation League, Touchstone worked for several Louisiana weeklies and owned his own printing company, the Bossier Press. The ADL reported:

> Articles in *The Councilor* have frequently attacked Jews in general and the ADL in particular. Touchstone's newspaper has stated that "The ADL (sometimes called the 'Russian Mafia') is composed of anti-Christ Khazars. . . ." In addition, ADL and "its international connections with communism" have figured prominently in anti-Semitic conspiracy stories published in *The Councilor.*

> Touchstone has been linked to Willis Carto's right-wing extremist group, Liberty Lobby. Besides holding a seat on their Board of Policy, he has been a featured speaker at several gatherings sponsored by Liberty Lobby. Touchstone himself has stated that, *"The Councilor and Liberty Lobby are on the same side 99 percent of the time."* Concerning the notorious anti-Semite Carto, Touchstone added, "I consider Willis Carto of Liberty Lobby one of the greatest living Americans. . . ."[13]

Roy Harris, of the Citizens' Councils of America, was a frequent writer for *The Councilor*. In a 1973 article entitled "Black Crime and Its Cause," he said:

> Negroes have been grabbing women and raping them in broad open daylight. They have been breaking into their homes and raping them. They have laid in wait in parking lots, in the shopping centers, and around the hospitals.

Nurses have been open targets at night for a series of rapes, muggings, beatings, and killings as they leave the hospitals. The women in this town are literally scared to death. . . .

Now, I blame the Supreme Court of the United States for all of this. . . . I indict the members of the Supreme Court for creating the conditions that produce this wave of crime of blacks against whites. . . . I indict the members of the Supreme Court for trying to force the integration of the white and black races.[14]

Readers were constantly reminded of something the paper predicted that later came true, or of some item that appeared in the pages of *The Councilor* before any other source printed it. In this respect it has been like most ideologically oriented publications. These claims usually appeared highly dubious to all but dedicated followers. In most instances it seemed that Touchstone had taken a leap of faith—that is, his news item did not support his previous "scoop." Typical among such articles was one entitled "We Told You So":

DALLAS—Five years ago *The Councilor* was the subject of bitter statements after it claimed that Ho Chi Minh was trained in New York City, as were Castro and Trotsky (Bronstein). No other news media would print this fact. But a few weeks ago wire service stories about the death of Ho mentioned that he was, indeed, a former resident of the United States—New York City, to be specific.[15]

Most political scientists and historians of our acquaintance have long known that Ho once lived in New York. Does this prove that he was "trained" there? Such an article smacks of the old charge that instrumental in the Russian Revolution were "260 Jewish assassins trained on the lower east side of New York." This, along with obsessing over the fact that Trotsky's real name was Bronstein, illustrates Touchstone's subtle anti-Semitism. Another illustration of his anti-Jewish bias appeared in the June 22, 1970, issue: "Most of the people in the business of importing Iron Curtain hams do not eat ham." He probably was not referring to Muslims. . . .

George Wallace for President

The Councilor was one of the first publications to support George Wallace for president, and probably the first to sell Wallace-for-President license plates. Also sold was "Squeeze Play," a protective device that directs a disabling chemical into the face of a would-be attacker. The advertisement claimed the chemical to be more effective than tear gas, marking the potential assailant with a special dye for later identification but causing no permanent damage.

Possibly even more reliable than George Wallace (in the eyes of Ned Touchstone) was Congressman John Rarick of Louisiana, who had right extremist connections throughout America. Rarick probably read more extremist literature into the *Congressional Record* than any congressman of the latter half of the twentieth century. Another reliable friend of Touchstone was Westbrook Pegler, a well-known columnist who after leaving the Birch magazine *American Opinion* in the early 1960s, wrote regularly for *The Councilor* until his death in mid-1969. Mr. Pegler once stated that hate was a strong motivating force in his life.

Often, extremist groups and publications may be characterized by the books they recommend (although a certain restraint needs to be applied to avoid jumping to unfair conclusions as in the case, for example, of a group that offers books representing all sides of an issue, including the extremes). This applies to *The Councilor,* whose list of advertised books sold through an in-house bookselling operation called the National Biographic Society, includes the following titles, most of which are devoted to conspiracy theories associated with the far right:

- *The Red Network* by Elizabeth Dilling
- *The Strange Death of Marilyn Monroe* by Frank Capell
- *The Clansman* by Thomas Dixon
- *Occult Theocrasy* by Lady Queensborough
- *Death of a Nation* by John Stormer
- *The Road Ahead* by John T. Flynn
- *Antisemitism* by Bernard Lazare

In our opinion *The Councilor* appealed to people intellectually and economically a cut above the average Klansman. We also believe this paper's influence was greater than its approximately 50,000 paid circulation—it claimed a readership of over 200,000—although in the final analysis its influence was nil by the early eighties, when it ceased publication. The influence of Citizens' Councils is basically dead, except for a few small groups that continue to use the name or some variation of it. *The Citizen* was still being published in the late 1980s. Its circulation was down to a few thousand and its previous stridency was scarcely in evidence.

NOTES

1. George Thayer, *The Farther Shores of Politics: The American Political Fringe Today* (New York: Simon & Schuster, 1967), 107–108.

2. Seymour Martin Lipset and Earl Raab, *The Politics of Unreason* (Chicago: University of Chicago Press, 1978), 277.

3. Francis M. Wilhoit, *The Politics of Massive Resistance* (New York: George Braziller, 1973), 111.

4. Kenneth O'Reilly, *Racial Matters: The FBI's Secret File on Black America, 1960–1972* (New York: The Free Press, 1989), 201.

5. Thayer, 105.

6. Quoted in Dan Wakefield, *Revolt in the South* (New York: Grove Press 1960), 57.

7. Rev. G.T. Gillespie, D.D., "A Christian View on Segregation," *The Citizen* (February 1973).

8. Thayer, 277.

9. Milton Ellerin, "Rightist Extremism," *American Jewish Year Book* (Philadelphia: Jewish Publication Society, 1966), 199.

10. Thayer, 123.

11. Mark Sherwin, *The Extremists* (New York: St. Martin's Press, 1963), 160–61.

12. *The Councilor* (May 3, 1969).

13. Anti-Defamation League, *Extremism on the Right* (New York: The League, 1983), 138.

14. Roy Harris, "Black Crime and Its Cause," *The Councilor* (July 7, 1973).

15. *The Councilor* (October 1, 1969).

White Power and the American Nazi Party

GEORGE LINCOLN ROCKWELL

George Lincoln Rockwell was the leader of the American Nazi Party, a small far-right group that was active during the 1950s and 1960s. His flamboyant activism garnered much public attention—which many analysts believe made the U.S. Nazi movement appear more organized than it actually was. Rockwell was assassinated by one of his own lieutenants in 1967, and is today considered a seminal historical figure by many white separatist organizations. In the following selection, excerpted from his 1967 book *White Power*, Rockwell calls for white Americans to unite and fight against the "mob rule" of Jews and nonwhites. He discusses the steps that he believes whites must take to save their race and take control of the nation and the world.

Make no mistake about it, I am advocating total and complete WHITE POWER in this world!

White men can no longer shilly-shally around with compromises and half-hearted measures to protect their own lives and interests. What we face is not a social, philosophical, economic, religious or territorial battle, but a struggle between QUALITY—the elite, but minority, White Race—against QUANTITY, the vast swarms of sub-human scum who have been gathered up under the banners of Jewish Marxism to be used as a giant battering ram against the White Race.

Our beleaguered Race will organize itself and fight for its own survival, or it will be inundated by the scum of the earth.

If we continue to hesitate, to rationalize, and to temporize with half-hearted measures, we will be obliterated from the face of this planet. This is truly "SCUM POWER" with a vengeance—like some horrible multiplication of roaches who, if there be only enough of them, can literally smother the greatest thinker or fighter in history—the scum of the world are gathering for the attack. *There are seven of them for every one of us!*

The only answer to SCUM POWER must be, and is, WHITE POWER. The power of the elite of the world, the White human beings who have already proved their natural, God-given superiority over this gathering swarm of scum, must drive it back, re-establish order and culture in the world, and maintain that order the only way order has ever been maintained—BY FORCE!

Today, there is no segment of the White Race left on earth with the *possibility* of turning back the scum except the White Men of the United States of America.

America is *the only* nation, as a matter of cold *fact* with the PHYSICAL power to master the scum. The center of Jewish power and money is *here* in New York City, U.S.A.—not Moscow, and not even Jerusalem. And the American working man and farmer *still* has in him the good and wholesome racial instincts of our ancestors who, time after time, drove back the mongrel hordes by sheer force of guts and will.

HOW EUROPE VIEWS AMERICA

I am well aware of the upwelling of revulsion which comes over many Europeans at the thought of the sort of "Americans" they have seen and experienced ever being able to re-establish Western Culture. And they can hardly be blamed. "American" representatives in Europe today are, for the most part, JEWS. The "American" foreign policy they have seen, which destroyed their countries, slaughtered their people, and turned half of Europe over to Communism, and which today continues to give aid and comfort to White Men's enemies while destroying their friends, was and is directed, inspired and instigated by JEWS.

In short, Europeans have seen America only through Jewish eyes—they have seen "Americans" who are not Americans at all, but Jews.

But my fellow White Men of Europe, believe me when I tell you that America is brimming over with good and brave men—men who share your blood, and who will bring honor to our race when *finally* they see the urgent necessity of rolling up their sleeves for an all-out fight.

But aside from that point, the eternal jealousies, rivalries, and blood feuds between segments of the White Race must be STOPPED—as a matter of strategic necessity—not to be continued for the benefit of united world Jewry.

White Men of Europe: put aside, if you can, the memory of two world wars in which we joined hands with our mortal enemies to slaughter your finest young men—we too shed our blood in those unholy wars. Forgive us for being so blind—for turning the deadly power of our might against you, instead of the Jewish Communism that is now devouring us all. Forgive us for the misery and degradation we forced upon you, and join us in a last ditch fight for our race and respective nations.

THIS TIME it will be different!

THIS TIME we shall stand together as brothers against a common foe.

THIS TIME the traitors will find no White Man anywhere who will listen to their lies and fight their battles for them.

THIS TIME we shall have no mercy for those who have caused untold suffering among our people; we shall give no quarter to those who have lived among us for no purpose other than to destroy us.

THIS TIME—together—WE SHALL DRIVE THE BAS-TARDS TO THE WALL! . . .

THE OBSTACLE TO VICTORY

TV, radio, movies, books, magazines, newspapers, schools, and even our own government officials, tell us constantly and repeatedly that it isn't "nice" to believe an African ape is not our equal—albeit the facts conclusively prove our superiority in all matters pertaining to a civilized society. It isn't "nice," we're taught to believe, to want our blood line kept pure—to want our grandchildren WHITE. It isn't "nice" to point to the filth, immorality, crime and disease that move into a neighborhood on the heels of Black "neighbors." It isn't "nice" to want our children educated on their own level, instead of being held down to that of the stupid Black. It isn't "nice," we are told, because it isn't "fair."

WHITES MUST UNITE

But let's turn it around.

Is it "nice" to have our women live in constant fear of being raped or murdered by a Black ape on the rampage? Is it "nice" to have our children adopting the language, attitudes and morals of sub-human scum? Is it "nice" to have our men competing with illiterates for their livelihood—and having the illiterates come out on top? Is it "nice" to tolerate taxes and inflationary prices to support the multiplication of Black scum, when it drives our mothers from the home and family into the factories? Is it "nice" to leave our children the inheritance of a world governed by alien scum?

HELL NO, IT ISN'T NICE—and it isn't fair.

You're a slave in your own country, White Man. Each year you get to keep less of the fruits of your labor; each year it gets more difficult to carry the burden the aliens have placed upon you; each year the cheap labor of aliens makes your future less secure; each year you retreat a few steps more into the world of slavery.

Where will it all end? I'LL TELL YOU—it will end with the complete and total annihilation of "Whitey."

STOP rationalizing a situation you *know* to be deadly serious. STOP temporizing with half-way measures in a situation that *screams* for decisive action. STOP using business, social etiquette, family and security as an excuse for downright cowardly behaviour. If you hesitate very much longer, the fight will be over—and the White Man will have lost!

STAND UP AND FIGHT! . . .

WE MUST UNITE AS A SOLID BLOC AGAINST THOSE WHO ARE DETERMINED TO "GET WHITEY!"

And to do that, there is a self-evident *truth* that must be recognized.

There exists in America today a state of almost total ANARCHY.

This is the era of MOB POWER.

If you have a mob behind you, you can get away, literally, with murder—as the Africans prove to us every summer.

If you do *not* have a mob, you can be a very Saint, and you will wind up beaten into physical and financial submission to those who *do* have a mob.

Until we realize this fact—that this is an era of ANARCHY, and that the only leader who now has any chance of DOING anything is the man with the mob—we will remain forever an eternally retreating society of hand-wringing groaners, pressed ever backward by the oncoming enemy.

In short, the problem before us is to form a WHITE MOB!

All the tactics of Adolf Hitler were realistically based on a recognition of that same sad fact in mob-ruled Germany.

When the enemy uses brass knuckles, you are whipped before you start if you are too chicken to put on a pair yourself.

Our enemies are beating us to DEATH with mobs, and unless we can find a way to build a bigger, better, tougher, and more powerful mob than theirs, we will be crushed and our country and race wiped out. The mob of scum now running wild, with the politicians all chasing after the scum, hat-in-hand, begging for their votes, will not be stopped by anything short of an angry, determined, *and organized* WHITE MOB. . . .

THE FIRST STEP

The first step toward forming our own WHITE mob is to start sticking together AS A RACE as the Jews and Negroes stick together.

When a Jew joins a "Civil Rights" march, or publicly advocates "VICTORY FOR THE VIET CONG," he doesn't lose his job or suffer persecution by his fellow Jews—he is PRAISED as a spokesman for "peace" and "Brotherhood."

And when a Negro shouts "KILL WHITEY," and leads a riot that terrorizes a whole city, he doesn't lose his job (if he has one), nor do his fellow Negroes criticize him as an "extremist"—he is a HERO fighting for *their* Cause, and is greeted with shouts of approval.

But when a WHITE MAN *publicly* displays his objection to the treason and mayhem that is now commonplace across America, he is attacked from every side as a "bigot" and a "hatemonger"—NOT just by the Jews, Negroes and Communists he opposes, but *by his own White people.*

SUCH INSANITY HAS GOT TO STOP!

If a White Man is brave enough to physically attack TRAITORS who are burning our American flag while waving the flag of our enemy, APPLAUD HIM—and if he works for you, and a Jew threatens to take his business and go elsewhere if you don't fire him, TELL THE JEW TO TAKE HIS BUSINESS AND GO TO HELL!

STOP letting arrogant Jews terrorize you into passive submission.

STOP letting Jew propaganda stampede you into attacking your own people.

STOP groveling for a piece of *your own* pie—stand up and TAKE IT! Unite as one people against a common enemy—that's the FIRST step in forming a realistic opposition to SCUM POWER.

THE SECOND STEP

The second step will be easy after the first step is done.

When White Men no longer have to fear the scorn of *their own* people, they will step forward by the hundreds of thousands to shout "WHITE POWER" in a roar that will be heard around the world. Already men of courage are letting their voices be heard; already thousands of White men and women have met the enemy in the streets to defy him to go further—in Chicago, the roar of "WHITE POWER" was deafening as the men and women of Cicero courageously declared their intent to STOP the Negroes dead in their tracks.

Perhaps it isn't "nice" to merge into a mob of thousands, shouting "WHITE POWER" in answer to those who are shouting "BLACK POWER," but neither is it nice to be over-run by a mob of savage Blacks. And we're faced with the hard: either/or.

Millions of White Americans are ready to fight, but they feel alone against the overpowering weight of the Federal Government and its SCUM MOB.

The only thing needed to make them an integral part of their people's march toward WHITE POWER in America is to REACH them, and then to ORGANIZE them into a force to be reckoned with.

It isn't enough to have millions of irate people who are ready to fight. If they are disorganized, the momentum of their anger will soon fade into nothingness against the highly organized might of the SCUM POWER.

To organize millions of people, we need PEOPLE—people who are fearless, who are dedicated, and who have few respon-sibilities to tie them down. We need YOUNG people to meet the enemy in the street, YOUNG people to go into areas of chaos and lead *our* people in concerted action when danger threatens: and YOUNG people to inspire the young White boys who have drifted into the degeneracy created by alien scum.

That's the second step and if these young men don't have to face persecution by their own people: if they can feel the WARMTH of a solid people behind them, the step will be easy. Young men are naturally eager for adventure and chal-lenge—they will storm into our ranks by the thousands *if only* we will stand behind them with pride. . . .

THE THIRD STEP

But people cannot be organized in vast numbers with any de-gree of success without MONEY—and that's the third and last step toward VICTORY over an enemy that *thinks* it has us whipped.

Since the day I hung up the Swastika in defiance of the filthy Communist Jews who were slowly but surely destroying the fiber of my people and the foundation of my country, MONEY—or the lack of it—has caused more problems, created more catastrophes, and rendered more plans unworkable, than all the obstacles that have been thrown in my path by the combined efforts of Jewish swine and Black scum. . . .

WITHOUT MONEY, the Party has gone as far as it can go in the creation of a *realistic* movement toward WHITE POWER in this world.

NOW WE MUST HAVE MONEY!

And if we are to be absolutely realistic, we must have LOTS of money.

The masses of White people are ready to fight—they've had ENOUGH of "niggers," and though they know little of the Jewish manipulation of their economy, they've had ENOUGH of burdensome taxation and ever-increasing inflation.

But we're in a Jewish-built circle insofar as we lack the MEANS to REACH those people.

. . . [My new] book [*White Power*] is part of the answer to that Jewish-built circle. I found with my first book that there were enough people of means, who also had the guts to read such a "controversial" book, and the intelligence to comprehend its message, to give us the financial strength to get this far.

I am confident that . . . [my] new book will take us the next step.

The Formula for Success

I believe I will be able to make at least a FEW men and women of vision see that there is a FORMULA for success in fighting the Jews and their "scum power," and that we alone have proven our ability to make that formula WORK.

The formula has been tested against the enemy. It WORKS! If we, who make up the majority in this nation, follow it to its end, we will gain LEGAL POLITICAL POWER in America—and White Men the world over will breathe a sigh of relief.

Though we must use tactics which are repugnant to the civilized mind of the White Man TO WIN political power, our intentions are, and must be, to establish the very opposite of the conditions which exist today.

We intend, as I have set forth in hundreds of pages of [my] book, to establish a government of NATURAL ORDER, a government *precisely* like that set up by the Founding Fathers of America; one which might best be called an "Authoritarian Republic."

The Laws of the Tribe, raised to the noble level of WHITE MEN, must be applied to any successful society and government, *and they were,* by the men who gave us America.

They did NOT set up a "democracy," precisely to avoid the danger of the mobs now running riot all over America.

They set up a REPUBLIC, in which the people choose REPRESENTATIVES—and the representatives, in an orderly manner, carry on the business of government.

They set up the machinery to choose REAL leaders, not the richest billionaires who could afford the best advertising agency, write the best jingles for TV, and perhaps do a little Hollywood jig to show "talent."

And the leaders they chose were never crawling curs, begging for the favor of transitory mobs. Washington had dignity; he was a man of natural, spiritual AUTHORITY; a man in whom every other man sensed leadership and authority.

We thus had a REPUBLIC, ruled not by a dictator, but by a man of unquestionable AUTHORITY, checked by a written constitution.

We believe that the original, NATURAL government of the USA was what would be called totally FASCIST—"racist" and National Socialist—but that that great and noble government has been so wrenched, and so perverted, by a packed Supreme Court and corrupt legislators and executives, that it will take a CONSTITUTIONAL CONVENTION to restore our original, natural, and honest government.

We believe, for instance, that no Jew and no Negro can be "citizens" of a White country without bringing about the ultimate downfall of that country. They have shown by their long continued actions that their entire spirits are alien and hostile AND DANGEROUS to the survival of the White people who are their hosts. We intend to get authority from the PEOPLE to revoke the citizenship of Jews, Negroes, and other non-Whites—and to make that a part of our Constitution.

When the National Socialist White People's Party is elected to power in a free election, we shall immediately remove all non-citizens from positions where they can control the thoughts or actions of the people, particularly from the press, government, education, entertainment and courts.

We shall investigate, try, and execute all Jews and non-Jews proved to have taken part in Marxist or Zionist plots of treason against their nations or humanity.

We shall establish an International Jewish Control Authority to carry out the above measures on a world-wide basis, to protect the rare honest Jew from the wrath of the people newly awakened to the truth about the Jews, and to make a long-term, scientific study to determine if the Jewish virus is a matter of environment and can be eliminated by education and training, or if some other method must be developed to render Jews harmless to society.

On the subject of the Negro, we have long made our position clear —*America must be all White; Blacks must be deported!* . . .

AN INTERNATIONAL RESPONSIBILITY

We shall assist all White people to throw off the yoke of Jewish oppression and establish their own free National Socialist governments.

We shall abolish the Marxist United Nations, and establish in its stead an organic Union of Free Enterprise National Socialist States, with a world police force to maintain order among the non-White peoples who still are unable to govern themselves. When the White Race is once more in control of its own destiny, it will then be able to adopt a sane policy of international responsibility that will bring the blessings of *real* peace and political sanity to the peoples of the earth. . . .

An All White America

An ALL WHITE AMERICA is *not* just a dream with no basis in reality!

WHITE POWER is *not* a goal with no possibility of attainment!

White people *are* the overwhelming majority in America. Therefore, White people *can* make WHITE POWER a reality in their own domain.

It is *not* "inevitable" that America fall into the hands of alien scum, or that Americans submit to alien insults.

But the time is not far off when it *will* be inevitable!

"KILL WHITEY" is not an idle threat.

The colored races of the world are gathering for the attack—armed with the weapons and knowledge of the White Man.

The Jews, sensing victory within their grasp, are becoming more arrogant every day.

Will you FIGHT, White Man? Or will you lay down your riches and even your lives for the momentary pleasures you are able to elicit from the Jews?

White Men around the world are waiting to see if America will lead the way, or if Americans, fearful of soiled hands, will allow the greatest Race on this planet to vanish into the ashes of history.

I've made my decision. What is yours?

CHAPTER 4

WHITE SEPARATIST MOVEMENTS OF THE LATE TWENTIETH CENTURY

AMERICAN
SOCIAL
MOVEMENTS

An Overview of the Radical Right Wing

JEFFREY KAPLAN

This 1995 article by journalist Jeffrey Kaplan, originally published in the *Christian Century*, presents a broad overview of radical right-wing groups of the late twentieth century—including various Klan, neo-Nazi, and Holocaust revisionist organizations. Writing in the wake of the April 1995 Oklahoma City bombing, Kaplan surmises that while the Klan is in decline, the threat posed by neo-Nazis and racist skinheads is difficult to determine. *The Turner Diaries*, a novel by neo-Nazi leader William Pierce about a violent white separatist revolution, is alleged to have inspired Timothy McVeigh to bomb the Oklahoma City federal building, but it is impossible to know whether radicals will increasingly engage in antigovernment violence. Kaplan concludes that dialogue is needed to combat radical right-wing paranoia as well as government suppression of dissenting groups.

T he siege of the Branch Davidian compound in Waco, Texas, by officials of the federal Bureau of Alcohol, Tobacco and Firearms [BATF] reached its fiery denouement on April 19, 1993. Americans expressed sadness for the tragic fate of the children, but the consensus was that cult members had in some way got what they deserved. In the more distant reaches of American life, however, quite another message was received. To many adherents of the radical right wing, the Waco raid offered proof that the U.S. government had declared open season on its citizens.

Paranoia writ large? Perhaps. But the radical right viewed Waco in the light of a series of confrontations between federal officers and adherents of right-wing causes. The names of

Excerpted from "A Guide to the Radical Right," by Jeffrey Kaplan, *Christian Century*, August 2, 1995. Copyright © 1995 by *Christian Century*. Reprinted with permission.

130 • THE WHITE SEPARATIST MOVEMENT

Gordon Kahl, Arthur Kirk, Robert Mathews and David Moran are unknown to most Americans (with the possible exception of Kahl, about whom a television movie was made), but they are instantly familiar throughout the radical right as the names of right-wing leaders killed in confrontations with the federal government. From the siege of the Covenant, Sword and the Arm of the Lord's compound in Missouri, to the federal attack on Randy Weaver's cabin in Idaho, to the conflagration at Waco, there has been an escalation in the use of force against inhabitants of America's cultural fringes. It seems that paranoids have real enemies.

THE MILITIA MOVEMENT

Yet the impact of Waco was different from that of the earlier confrontations. Almost before the ashes of the Davidian compound had cooled, a video began to circulate warning of more Wacos to come and urging the faithful to organize in self-defense lest the FBI and the BATF pick them off one by one. Linda Thompson, the producer and star of "Waco, the Big Lie," is in a sense the mother of the militia movement.

The ideological hallmark of the citizen militias is their sense that change is rarely for the good and never the result of chance. Any deviation from the "golden age" of America's past has been the result of a conscious, malignant design. From this belief flow extravagant conspiracy scenarios.

The various militia manuals, videos, newsletters and computer files supplement this conspiratorial mind-set with a cornucopia of details drawn from both scripture and right-wing politics. Computer chip technology is equated with the "Mark of the Beast." The tireless search for "black helicopters" and "blue helmets" is mingled with an interest in flying saucers and natural disasters. The message is that time is short and cataclysm imminent. Against this daunting array of modern demons, the men and women of the militias take refuge in biblical assurances of ultimate victory and in a constitutional fundamentalism which treats the Declaration of Independence and the American Constitution as holy writ.

The militia groups have studiously eschewed violence. Theirs is a call to vigilance and preparation for the coming time of tribulation. The militia groups are ad hoc collections of part-time enthusiasts whose backgrounds and opinions are startlingly diverse. Women, a small number of Jews, and members of racial and ethnic minorities can be counted among their number.

This quest for end-times unity is reflected in Mark Zorky's opening remarks to a recent Michigan Militia meeting: "We accept all races, all religions into the militia and if you are in any way bigoted or prejudiced or have hatred in your heart towards other races and religions, you are asked to leave and not join." Nonetheless, the gatherings of these weekend warriors are a primary opportunity for other radical right-wing appeals. In this respect, the militia groups may prove to be an important point of entry to the wider world of the radical right wing—just as was the tax protest movement of the 1980s.

NORTH AMERICA'S RADICAL RIGHT

The primary constituents of the radical right wing in North America may be classified as follows: Ku Klux Klan groups, Christian Identity believers, neo-Nazi groups, adherents of re-constructed traditions, and idiosyncratic sectarians. There are also single-issue constituencies and what can be called the "young toughs" of the movement. All these groups share a belief in a "golden age," scripturalism, a Manichaean [dualistic] worldview, the perception of a "theft of culture," a conspiratorial view of history, a vision of their group as a "righteous remnant," an apocalyptic analysis of society and a concomitant chiliastic [millenialist] dream. This explains the tendency of adherents to belong to more than one group or belief system. Indeed, this community of seekers is embarked on an endless quest for the ultimate "answer" to society's ills. Yet some groups are more susceptible to calls for violence than others. The more distant a particular group is from the values and beliefs of the mainstream society, the more difficult it is for adherents to moderate or abandon their beliefs.

• *Ku Klux Klan groups:* No organization elicits a more negative reaction from the general public than the Ku Klux Klan. The deeply rooted fear many Americans feel for the Klan at once attracts and bedevils Klan recruits. Attraction to the Klan's mystique often wanes when new members realize that virtually any public Klan activity will be met by a far greater crowd of counterdemonstrators. Worse, federal agencies have had little difficulty in infiltrating Klan ranks, making covert Klan operations a dubious venture. Hate crime regulations assure convicted Klansmen of lengthy incarceration. In addition, the successful use of civil litigation initiated by such watchdog organizations as the Klanwatch Project of the Southern Poverty Law Center on behalf of victims of Klan violence has been successful in putting out of business those Klans that do perpetrate acts of violence.

Given these powerful disincentives to violence, it is not surprising that the already fragmented Klans in North America would engage in bitter polemics over the use of violence. Emerging from this debate are two very different approaches. On the one hand, such firebrands as Louis Beam of Texas and Dennis Mahon of Oklahoma issue a call to revolutionary violence. On the other hand, Arkansas-based Thomas Robb attempts to market the Klan as a civil rights group for white people modeled on the example of Martin Luther King!

Beam aims to revitalize the fragmented Klan through the institution of what he and the late Robert Miles styled the Fifth Era Klan, a unified and revitalized Klan movement which would serve as the vanguard of the revolutionary right. The futility of this quest is evident in the fact that Mahon despaired of the movement and opted to join Tom Metzger's White Aryan Resistance (WAR). According to all observers, the Klan is a waning force.

IDENTITY AND NEO-NAZI GROUPS

• *Christian Identity:* Perhaps the fastest-growing segment of the radical right is based on a peculiar theological claim: that the most egregious "theft of culture" in human history was perpetrated by Satan and the Jews to dispossess the Anglo-Saxon and kindred peoples of their birthright.

Identity theology is an example par excellence of the radi-

The Turner Diaries

The Turner Diaries, a science-fiction novel written by National Alliance leader William Pierce, is alleged to have influenced Timothy McVeigh to bomb the Oklahoma City federal building in 1995. In the following excerpt, militant white separatists bomb the national headquarters of the FBI.

October 13, 1991. At 9:15 yesterday morning our bomb went off in the FBI's national headquarters building. Our worries about the relatively small size of the bomb were unfounded; the damage is immense. We have certainly disrupted a major portion of the FBI's headquarters operations for at least the next several weeks, and it looks like we have also achieved our goal of wrecking their new computer complex. . . .

George and I headed for the FBI building in the car, with Henry following in the truck. We intended to park near the 10th Street freight entrances and watch until the freight door to the basement level was opened for another truck, while Henry waited with "our" truck two blocks away. We would then give him a signal via walkie-talkie.

As we drove by the building, however, we saw that the basement entrance was open and no one was in sight. We signalled Henry and kept going for another seven or eight blocks, until we found a good spot to park. Then we began walking back slowly, keeping an eye on our watches.

We were still two blocks away when the pavement shuddered violently under our feet. An instant later the blast wave hit us—a deafening "ka-whoomp," followed by an enormous roaring, crashing sound, accentuated by the

cal right's apocalyptic millenarianism, as well as of its chiliastic dreams. It appears to have a unique ability to meet the need of the racialist right for spirituality, fellowship and ritual in the

higher-pitched noise of shattering glass all around us.

The plate glass windows in the store beside us and dozens of others that we could see along the street were blown to splinters. A glittering and deadly rain of glass shards continued to fall into the street from the upper stories of nearby buildings for a few seconds, as a jet-black column of smoke shot straight up into the sky ahead of us. . . .

The scene in the courtyard was one of utter devastation. The whole Pennsylvania Avenue wing of the building, as we could then see, had collapsed, partly into the courtyard in the center of the building and partly into Pennsylvania Avenue. A huge, gaping hole yawned in the courtyard pavement just beyond the rubble of collapsed masonry. . . .

Overturned trucks and automobiles, smashed office furniture, and building rubble were strewn wildly about—and so were the bodies of a shockingly large number of victims. Over everything hung the pall of black smoke, burning our eyes and lungs and reducing the bright morning to semi-darkness. . . .

[Henry] waited by a public phone booth a block away until one minute before the explosion was due, then placed a call to the newsroom of the *Washington Post*. His brief message was: "Three weeks ago you and yours killed Carl Hodges in Chicago. We are now settling the score with your pals in the political police. Soon we'll settle the score with you and all other traitors. White America shall live!"

That should rattle their cage enough to provoke a few good headlines and editorials!

Andrew MacDonald (pseudonym of William Pierce), *The Turner Diaries*, 1978.

context of a Christianity shorn of its Jewish roots. Identity doctrine gives shape and substance to the conspiratorial suspicions of the faithful remnant. Identity provides the key to unlocking the mysteries of past, present and future while offering the faithful an explanation for their current perception of dispossession. Identity apprises believers of the golden era that lasted until the "satanic Jews" robbed them of the knowledge of their covenantal birthright, and it assures them of a future of happiness and terrestrial power.

• *Neo-Nazi groups:* The highly disparate world of neo-Nazi groups in North America is notable for both its high-profile activism and its minuscule size. National Socialism [NS] in America remains influential thanks to the efforts of its few effective propagandists who have proved to be a valuable resource for a broad spectrum of radical right-wing appeals.

If the radical right is fractious, however, National Socialism is fratricidal. As West Virginia Nazi figure George Dietz has observed, the movement boasts "a lot of little Fuhrers with no brains and lots of guts." It is a highly idiosyncratic collection of leaders scattered around the country whose unenviable task it is to lead a tiny and unsavory band of followers toward the dream of revolution and the institution of a New Order. The movement is bitterly divided between the conservative majority that favors mass action and the careful building of a broad, revolutionary coalition, and the minority that favors immediate revolutionary violence on the model of left-wing guerrilla movements of the 1960s. In either case, the dream is millennial. George Lincoln Rockwell's successor, Matt Kohl, recalls: "Like a true disciple, he [Rockwell] would be propagating the Millennial Idea as the rallying banner of an embattled race."

The single most influential neo-Nazi in North America is National Alliance leader William Pierce. It was Pierce, writing under the pseudonym of Andrew Macdonald, who authored *The Turner Diaries,* which has become a kind of textbook for the violent fringe of the radical right wing. The novel is about an underground group that kills Jews, blacks, and those whites guilty of "race mixing," as part of an effort to overthrow a Jewish-dominated government. Timothy McVeigh, a suspect in the Oklahoma City bombing [eventually convicted and sentenced to death], reportedly not only read *The Turner Diaries* but sold copies to friends and acquaintances.

Rick Cooper and Gerhard (Gary) Lauck do not approach the status of William Pierce. Both head National Socialist organizations which have no members. Yet both enjoy a certain degree of influence in National Socialist circles—Cooper in North America and Lauck abroad, especially in Germany. They approach NS doctrine from opposite poles. Where Cooper seeks to adapt NS principles to the creation of a small, separatist utopian communalism, Lauck unabashedly dreams of world revolution and pledges obeisance to the ghost of Adolf Hitler. Lauck is currently imprisoned in Denmark, facing extradition to Germany.

RECONSTRUCTED TRADITIONS

• *Odinism:* Reconstructed traditions are consciously modeled on idealized traditions of the past. In the world of the radical right, two reconstructed traditions have played important roles. Dualism, an elaborate construct based on Mountain Kirk (Church) impresario Robert Miles's Francophile fascination for the Cathari, a medieval French dualist sect, died with him in 1992. Odinism, however, remains vibrant and shows considerable potential for growth.

Odinism is a reconstruction of the Norse-Germanic pantheon. It links the racialist appeals of the radical right with the occult-magical themes of Wiccan witchcraft and neo-paganism. Odinists practice an imaginative blend of ritual magic, ceremonial forms of fraternal fellowship, and an ideological flexibility which allows for a remarkable degree of syncretism with other white supremacist concerns. Ironically, Odinists tend to subscribe to a number of beliefs which are explicitly Christian. Anti-Semitism would have been incomprehensible to the pagan Norse, as would the radical right's ubiquitous conspiratorial fantasies.

Odinism is becoming increasingly distinct from its counterpart, Asatru. Devotees of the same Norse-Germanic pantheon, Asatruers tend to eschew racist constructions of their tradition. The current constituency of racist Odinism is diverse. Best known is David Lane, a member of Robert Mathew's quixotic revolutionary group known as the Order. A variety of skinheads and more than a smattering of National Socialists also profess to be Odinists. Odinism travels well, linking adherents in North America with like-minded groups in Germany, southern Africa and Scandinavia.

• *Idiosyncratic sectarians and the Church of the Creator:* Idiosyncratic sectarians are an assortment of groups and individuals who have withdrawn to rural compounds or engaged in psychological withdrawal. The Church of the Creator [COC] is typical of groups making the latter move.

Individual survivalists and the "creators," as adherents of the Church of the Creator like to be called, have more in common than might seem to be the case. Both are composed of highly idiosyncratic individuals who profess fealty to no one. This might seem odd in the case of the "creators," who were originally headed by a charismatic and highly authoritarian leader. Despite some organizational trappings, however, the Church of the Creator remains a mail order ministry.

The COC centers on the belief that because Christianity is built upon the foundation of Judaism, it is anathema—as is the society which would embrace such a "Jewish fable." Following this line of reasoning, the "Pontifex Maximus," as COC founder Ben Klassen styled himself, deduced that if Christianity is built on a lie, then all religions must be false. Moreover, since the Jews are the source of all the lies of this world, all religions are Jewish creations constructed to enslave the world. Having rejected the existence of God or any other supernatural being, the COC offers instead Creativity—an odd blend of militant atheism, health faddism and scabrous racism. The Church of the Creator has declined in the U.S. following Ben Klassen's suicide, but it remains vibrant in Europe.

SINGLE-ISSUE RADICALS

• *Single-issue constituencies:* True single-issue constituencies are rare in the world of the radical right. The primary case of single-issue zealotry is the tax protest movement which held the fleeting attentions of such stalwarts as Robert Mathews and Posse Comitatus founder William Potter Gale. Few people have remained exclusively in the tax movement, however. For one thing, the Internal Revenue Service aggressively combats anything that smacks of tax resistance. Also, the literature of the tax protest movement is as arcane as the tax code. Unraveling these mysteries is a task for which few in this milieu are intellectually or temperamentally equipped. Finally, tax protesters who investigate the "truth" behind the government's policies are inevitably led to more interesting revelations. Who stands behind the bankers who profit from the "illegal" federal reserve system? It can only be those masters of financial chicanery, the Jews. Having made this deduction, the theorist then has a banquet of conspiratorial scenarios from which to choose.

Like tax protest, Holocaust revisionism requires a cadre of single-minded specialists. In this case, they are eager to comb the vast literature emanating from the Second World War in an effort to disprove the claim that the Nazi regime systematically exterminated Jews. In the revisionists' view, this was a lie perpetrated by Zionist Jews and elite Western co-conspirators in their quest to establish a Jewish homeland, extort financial support for that homeland, and discredit German National Socialism.

The epicenter of Holocaust revisionism is the Institute for Historical Review, which publishes the *Journal of Historical Review*. Revisionist Bradley Smith's tactic of placing advertisements in college newspapers throughout the U.S. has brought revisionism its greatest media exposure. Whether the advertisement is published or censored, the ensuing debate provides enormous publicity for the revisionist view.

Revisionists obsessively search for "long-suppressed" facts which will undermine the case against Nazi Germany. Revisionists believe that this Achilles' heel is historians' conventional claim that 6 million Jews were murdered by the Nazi regime. If this figure could be disproved, would that not plant a seed of doubt that perhaps all Holocaust claims are specious? The public would then see the Jew as does the revisionist—as a master conspirator. At a stroke, Jewish control of the U.S. government would be sundered, as would American support for the state of Israel.

• *Knuckle draggers:* A headline in the Klanwatch *Intelligence Report* reads: "West Coast Bomb and Assassination Plots Spearheaded by Racist Skinheads: Young White Supremacists Eager to Act on Violent Race War Fantasies of the Movement's Elders." The headline encapsulates some observers' fears that skinheads will place themselves under the command of veteran racist leaders in a terrorist campaign aimed at igniting a race war. The plot referred to allegedly centered on a planned bombing of a Los Angeles church whose parishioners included such black celebrities as Arsenio Hall and Dionne Warwick. Implicated in the plot were people affiliated with the racist skinhead organizations American Front and Fourth Reich Skins. Adding tantalizing hints of bigger game to be caught were the connections of members of the conspiracy to Tom Metzger's WAR and the Church of the Creator. The scenario is sobering.

It is difficult to assess how great a threat the skinhead movement represents. The Anti-Defamation League's estimate of skinhead numbers peaks at 3,500, and this does not differentiate between racist skins and apolitical or overtly antiracist skinheads. What is certain is that skinheads represent a population whose fealty is much sought after in the world of the radical right. What is equally certain from skinhead writings and white power music is that the skinhead population is very much aware of the attention it receives, and has little inclination to enlist in any particular leader's private army.

AVOIDING ANOTHER OKLAHOMA CITY

The literature emanating from the various outposts of the radical right wing has firmly condemned the bombing in Oklahoma City. These comments are accompanied, however, with assertions of understanding for the accused and claims that the bombing was inevitable given the increasing hostility of a government seen as the tool of a conspiratorial group of alien elites. The epithet ZOG (Zionist Occupation Government) is in this respect no mere rhetorical device, and it is through the lens of this alienation that the radical right's outrage over Waco can best be understood.

Will the radical right wing turn increasingly to acts of antistate violence? It is impossible to know for certain. The evolution of views on violence within the pro-life "rescue" movement perhaps suggests one scenario. When the rescue message went unheeded by both the churches and the larger society, and as punitive legislation increasingly forced all but the most committed of the rescue community to the sidelines, rescuers began to debate the utility of violence.

Then a peripheral member of the rescue community, Michael Griffin, acted upon this rhetoric and shot to death Dr. David Gunn. This act breached the barriers. Within two years Shelley Shannon and Paul Hill had taken up the gun, and a minority of the movement were applauding their acts.

Given the demonization which currently typifies our perception of the radical right—and its perception of us—it is possible that Timothy McVeigh will be remembered as the Michael Griffin of the radical right. This scenario is not inevitable, however.

Congress's invitation to high-profile militia leaders to testify before Congress in June 1995 was a promising start to breaking the cycle of right-wing suspicion and government suppression. Another healthy development is the convening of congressional hearings into Waco and Ruby Ridge. The recent demotion of an FBI official in the latter case is notable as well. In the end, a process of dialogue rather than punitive regulation or efforts to limit the protection of the First and Second Amendments will be the best way to avoid another Oklahoma City.

The Theology of the Christian Identity Movement

In the following piece Jerome Walters outlines the belief system common to several of today's religiously oriented white separatist groups. According to adherents of "Christian Identity," Adam and Eve were the first white humans, and the white race was specially chosen as God's people. Identity theology also claims that nonwhites are beings without souls who, along with the animals, were created before Adam. Jews are allegedly the descendants of Eve and a Satan-possessed nonwhite, and their existence is contrary to God's original plan. Racial mixing, therefore, is the "original sin" that led to the expulsion of whites from the Garden of Eden and the reason why whites today must fight for racial separation. Walters is the author of *One Aryan Nation Under God: Exposing the New Racial Extremists*, from which this selection is excerpted.

> *Remember that the Bible was written for only one race of people.*
> —Freeman Edict

Identity racism is shaped by a particular reading of the creation accounts in the first chapters of Genesis. Put together, these beliefs form a clear theology that is contrary to Judaism and Christianity. Here are some of Identity's core commitments:

1. The different races have their origins in separate creations by God (polygenesis).
2. People of color (nonwhites) were created before Adam

Excerpted from *One Aryan Nation Under God: Exposing the New Radical Extremists*, by Jerome Walters (Cleveland: Pilgrim Press, 2000). Copyright © 2000 by The Pilgrim Press. Reprinted with permission.

142 • THE WHITE SEPARATIST MOVEMENT

and Eve, are less endowed spiritually, and do not share in redemption.

3. Adam and Eve were the first white people created by God, were a race endowed with exceptional spiritual capacities, and were specially chosen by God; white descendants of Adam and Eve share these same capacities and election.

4. Present-day Jews are descendants of Satan and Eve and are fundamentally opposed to God and God's purposes.

5. Race mixing was the original sin in the Garden of Eden and the source of the white race's woes outside the garden, which led to the Flood—and the current need for racial separation.

THE BEASTS OF THE FIELD

Identity racism is convinced that the Bible is God's revelation concerning the races and that "the Bible was written for only one race of people."[1] To be sure, a wide spectrum of movements are counted in Identity—from those spearheaded by the former Grand Wizard of the Ku Klux Klan and politician David Duke to the founder and leader of Aryan Nations, Richard Girnt Butler. But they share this basic conviction and conclusion.

The groups that are in the Identity category, then, cannot be characterized as consisting of people who, in the words of one prominent Identity pastor, "fall into the religious right."[2] Their virulent racism clearly precludes this. Neither are they merely tax protesters or antigovernment activists, although many do protest taxes and often oppose the federal government. Identity churches and communities such as the Montana Freemen, Laporte Church of Christ in Colorado, and American Christian Ministries in Medford, Oregon, adhere to and live out of dehumanizing forms of racial theology. It can be shown that every other commitment they espouse—however unconnected from other parts of their agenda it may seem at first—flows from the belief that the Bible was written for the white race only.

Taking the narrative from Genesis in order, Identity extremism alleges that the first creation narrative (Gen. 1–2:4) is an account of God's creating inferior, *pre-Adamic* (that is, born before Adam) people of color. Such persons of color are less endowed spiritually and intellectually, they maintain, than the Adamic white race, which was placed later on earth.

But was not humankind created in the "image of God" (Gen. 1:27)? According to the Montana Freemen, this refers to the dark people of color: "The first men, both male and female, were created in God's shadow or image, dark color." Also, according to Identity doctrine, pre-Adamic people are without souls: "These men were created at the same time, male and female. . . . These men, males and females, did not receive the breath of life, or that special spirit, electrical energy, or a soul (Gen. 1:27)."[3] And because translations of this first creation account (Gen. 1–2:4) lack the distinctive words for the male and female (Adam and Eve) found in Genesis 2, these pre-Adamic people are claimed to somehow be more generic, "stamped out," and inferior to the Adamic white race. Also lifted from these early verses of Genesis is that people of color are called "beasts of the field" (Gen. 3:1 KJV). The non-Aryans, it is alleged, were created along with and are on the same level as animals such as cattle and birds; these "beasts" were "soulless people of color."

The search for references to "beasts of the field" elsewhere in the Bible, for them, seems to substantiate this interpretation. For example, in the laws of the book of Leviticus, bestiality, or sexual relations with an animal, is prohibited. Identity extremists interpret this as God's command forbidding Aryans to race mix. In fact, race mixing was punishable by death: "If a man lie with a beast [read: person of color], he shall surely be put to death: and ye shall slay the beast. And if a woman approach unto any beast, and lie down thereto, thou shalt kill the woman, and the beast" (Lev. 20:15–16 KJV). To lend a scientific aura to the biblical claims, racial extremists often cite evidence they claim is irrefutable. That this racial theology is ever disputed is looked upon as a ploy to raise up the "false doctrine" of the equality of races.

THE ADAMIC WHITE RACE

Turning to Genesis 2, Identity adherents assert that the Adamic white race was specially created, favored by God from the beginning. This creation account (Gen. 2:4–25), which follows the well-known seven-day creation story, is read as a fluid continuation of those seven days. It follows then that since "on the seventh day God finished the work that God had done, and God rested" (Gen. 2:2), Adam, the first white man, was "formed from the ground on the eighth day" of creation and placed by God in the cradle prepared for the white race. Adam was "the father of only one race on this earth, that is the Caucasian race": "We believe God chose unto himself a special race of people that are above all people upon the face of the earth. . . . We believe the White, Anglo-Saxon, Germanic and kindred people to be God's true, literal Children of Israel."[4] This main tenet of Identity, the "Israel Truth" that the white race was chosen from creation and constitutes biblical Israel, pervades most Identity works:

- The Israel Truth is the key that opens up the Bible from the first promise made at the Fall, until Jesus delivers up the finished Kingdom to the Father.[5]
- The key to understanding the Bible is the truth that we [read: the white race] are Israelites.[6]
- God breathed life into Adam (Gen. 2:7) "giving him a higher form of consciousness and distinguishing him from all the other races of the earth."[7]

In this second creation account (Gen. 2:4–25), the personal nouns Adam and Eve are used for the first time. The meaning of the Hebrew word for Adam is thought to support the divine elevation of the white race because, Identity adherents argue, "Adam . . . means: ruddy, to show blood in the face, flush or turn rosy, to be able to blush, to be fair."[8] The biblical account of creation expands around Adam (in Genesis 2), created by God's life-giving word, through the creation of all animals that God brings to Adam for names, until finally woman, Eve, is created and brought to Adam (Gen. 2:18–25).

THE TWO-SEED THEORY AND SATAN'S KIDS

The harmony of Adam and Eve's partnership and marriage is short-lived, however, because according to Identity doctrine, a satanic sexual seducer lurked in Eden (Gen. 3:1–7). This portion of Genesis is traditionally known as the Fall. But for Identity disciples, the two-seed theory of the origins of humankind emerges. "The serpent" appears on the scene (Gen. 3:1) and converses with Eve concerning the trees God planted in the center of the garden, and questions the prohibition by God concerning the fruit of the "tree of knowledge of good and evil." Eventually, both Adam and Eve disobey God, partake of the fruit, and are judged by God for their rebellion (or Fall).

The importance of Genesis 3—and more particularly Genesis 3:15—for Identity theology cannot be overstated. Addressed to the serpent and found in the judgment section of the narrative (3:14–19), Genesis 3:15 reads: "I will put enmity between you and the woman, and between your offspring and hers." Identity adherents assert that what is revealed in this verse is a genetic hatred between the Adamic white race and Satan's offspring, the Jews. The claim is that in the garden there was a "counterfeit incarnation" by Satan, whose plan was to perpetuate his own seed-line and whose descendants, contrary to God's plans, would pass themselves off as the true Israel of the Bible. The Identity book *The Two Seeds of Genesis 3:15* calls this verse "the key that unlocks the Bible."

> If you were to select one verse in the Bible that gives its most complete summary, Genesis 3:15 would be that verse. If you capture a vision of this verse and move forth conceptually . . . you will put all of the pieces of the puzzle together.

Identity asserts that there are two lines of descendants originating from Eve. Adam and Eve had sexual relations, they assert, and their offspring was Abel, who was killed by Cain and replaced by Seth. From Adam and in turn Seth's descendants came the white race, the true Israel, the chosen people of God: "The unconditional election of a people named Israel . . . from the race of Adam is a cornerstone of Bible teaching."[9] Because pure-blood descendants are from the seed-line of Adam, the first white man, these descendants are inherently good. But another seed-line originates in the garden, they say. Eve also had sexual relations with the serpent or a humanoid satanic being. The offspring of Eve and Satan was Cain, the first Jew, a literal child of Satan on earth. Cain and his offspring are genetically evil: "We believe in an existing being known as the Devil or Satan and called the Serpent . . . who has a literal seed or posterity in the earth . . . commonly called Jews today."[10]

According to this theory, the world contains descendants of Adam and descendants of Satan, a kind of incarnational dualism, good and evil right down on earth, which is the source of a life-and-death struggle between Satan's descendants and the children of God. (See diagram 1.) Racism and anti-Semitism have existed for centuries in one form and degree of severity or another. But one cannot dehumanize or demonize any human being more than this: "Cain, made in the image and likeness of Satan, took on the nature of Satan's evil and sinful ways. Cain was the personification of sin."[11] The claim is that

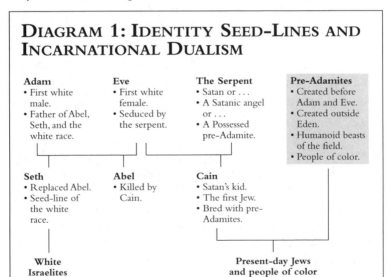

DIAGRAM 1: IDENTITY SEED-LINES AND INCARNATIONAL DUALISM

Adam
- First white male.
- Father of Abel, Seth, and the white race.

Eve
- First white female.
- Seduced by the serpent.

The Serpent
- Satan or . . .
- A Satanic angel or . . .
- A Possessed pre-Adamite.

Pre-Adamites
- Created before Adam and Eve.
- Created outside Eden.
- Humanoid beasts of the field.
- People of color.

Seth
- Replaced Abel.
- Seed-line of the white race.

Abel
- Killed by Cain.

Cain
- Satan's kid.
- The first Jew.
- Bred with pre-Adamites.

White Israelites

Present-day Jews and people of color

Good ——————— vs. ——————— Evil

present-day Jews are literally demonic, genetically and spiritually, and because of their heredity, are the natural enemies of
the white race. Identity adherents are essentially saying that
there are those who are outside the realm and power of God's
love and mercy given in Jesus Christ. Heaven has been assaulted by these new racial extremists, and hell opened ready
to receive its nonwhites; baptism cannot save the Jews, they
believe, because they are Satan's kids.

THE SERPENT

The sexual seduction that would lead to the satanic seed-line
begins with Genesis 3:1: "Now the serpent was more subtle
than any beast of the field which the Lord God had made"
(KJV). The word for "serpent"—using a very creative combination of etymology, Arabic, and word association—is concluded to be Satan, a lower helper of Satan such as a "handsome angel," or a two-legged "beast of the field" possessed by
Satan to do Satan's bidding. The pamphlet *In the Image of God*
concludes that the serpent was an exceptional "beast of the
field" used by Satan for evil purposes: "Satan made use of this
creature as the most proper instrument for the accomplishment
of his murderous purposes against the life and soul of man.
Under this creature he lay hid, and by this creature he seduced
our first parents. We have here a genuine clue in full support
of the deduction that [the serpent], a highly intelligent beast
of the field, was a purebred Negro."

One Identity interpreter confidently concludes, "Any other
interpretation for the serpent denies the reality of the Bible."[12]
And any other conclusion has elsewhere been described as
"undoubtedly the greatest hoax in history."[13] Having established
the sinister or satanic origin of the serpent and its humanoid
form, Identity regards as another key to interpretation the discussion of the trees in the center of the garden and the forbidden fruit from the tree of the knowledge of good and evil.

In Identity theology, the serpent as tempter becomes the
serpent as sexual seducer, developed with a metaphorical interpretation of the trees and fruit in the garden, the two trees

planted representing the bodily presence of God and Satan (Gen. 2:9): "The 'tree' in the garden was in fact the 'serpent,' a.k.a. Satan, the Dragon, the Devil, the Arch-Angel, Lucifer."[14] And Eve, like all women, it is asserted, in being susceptible to giving in to her lower faculties, chose the "tree" that was pleasant to the eyes, took, and ate. In the words of an Identity minister in a taped lecture: "It wasn't an apple in the hand of Eve as the so-called Christian churches claim, but it was a pear [read: pair] on the ground."[15] The Montana Freemen put it this way: "Now you can visualize a beautiful garden with two men in it one being Yhvh [God] (the tree of life) who was not strikingly handsome, the other man however, Satan (the tree of Knowledge, of both good and evil) was good looking and desirable to Eve, also good for food and eating or partaking of him." The Genesis narrative goes on to tell us that after Adam and Eve disobeyed God and partook of the forbidden fruit, their "eyes were opened"; they realized that they were naked and "sewed fig leaves together and made loincloths for themselves" (Gen. 3:7). Reasoning from the two-seed theory, Identity states, "If, as the so-called churches would have you believe, their sin was eating the forbidden fruit, why did they not put the fig leaf over their mouth?"

THE "ORIGINAL SIN"

Next, Adam and Eve are questioned by God (Gen. 3:11), and both point beyond themselves to assign the responsibility for their disobedience. Adam blames God and Eve, and in turn Eve blames the serpent, who "tricked" her (Gen. 3:13) or, Identity claims, sexually seduced her. For Identity, the sin in the garden that resulted in the fall of humankind and a broken relationship with God was not humankind's disobeying the word of God and wanting to be more like the Creator than like the creatures they were created to be. The sin in the garden was not Adam and Eve's inability to live out of trust. For Identity adherents, looking through the lens of the two-seed theory of the origins of humankind, the sin in the garden, the original sin, was race mixing—in Adolf Hitler's words, "blood sin and desecration of the race."

And the responsibility for this sin rests with Eve: "In original sin, Satan was able to physically seduce the woman Eve. . . . Cain was the bastard, spurious seed that resulted from their cohabitation."[16] Because Eve committed the great sin of race mixing, Eve, Adam, and the whole human race must face a battle with the seed of the serpent for the life of God's chosen white race. Adam's sin is explained in sexual terms as well, but it seems an afterthought to include him in the responsibility for the broken relationship with God. Identity theology claims that Adam's sin was to have sexual relations with Eve after she had defiled herself with Satan.

> What, then, was Adam's sin in having conjugal relations with his wife? First, Adam knew that the woman had been seduced by Satan. Second, Adam knew that the woman was fallen from glory and immortality and now existed in a body of sin. Third, Adam knew that to join with his wife in physical intimacy in her state of sin would incur the wrath of God.[17]

A simple reading of Genesis 4:1 would seem to reveal that Cain could be none other than Adam and Eve's offspring. Genesis 4:1 reads, "Now the man knew his wife Eve, and she conceived and bore Cain, saying, 'I have produced a man with the help of God.'" Even an Identity adherent admits that "at first glance, one would assume that Cain was the offspring of this man and wife."[18] First, that the Bible states only once that Adam knew (in this case the verb refers to sexual relations) his wife (Gen. 4:1) is taken as proof that Adam was the father of only one child, Abel, and not Cain. One explanation offered by Identity is that Eve was deceived by Satan into thinking that she had begotten a son with a messenger from God, an angel of light (see 2 Cor. 11:14), who was in fact Satan in disguise. Cain and Abel are related, Identity adherents would say, but only through their mother. They are the offspring of different fathers.

All of the punishments given by God because of Eve's disobedience are integrated into Identity interpretation. For example, the serpent was cursed to crawl upon its belly and to eat the dust all the days of its life (Gen. 3:14). "If the serpent was a snake," one Identity interpretation asks, "why would God say that he was to crawl on his belly, he must not have crawled before the event."[19] And the perpetual enmity between the offspring of the serpent and the offspring of Eve (Gen. 3:15) represents the division among races, and for some Identity adherents, divine sanction to do battle.

THE FIRST JEW: A MURDERER AND A LIAR

Genesis 4 contains the story of the brothers (half brothers, Identity would assert) Cain and Abel (Gen. 4:1–26) and the further unfolding of the histories of the seed-line of Adam and the seed-line of Satan. In the course of time Cain and Abel bring offerings before God, Cain from the fruit of the ground, and Abel from the firstlings of his flock. The Bible tells us that "God had regard for Abel and his offering, but for Cain and his offering God had no regard" (Gen. 4:4–5).

Through the lens of the two-seed theory, it stands to reason that God would reject Cain's offering; Cain was the offspring of Satan and at enmity with God and God's purposes. Satan, through Cain and his descendants, was out to thwart the purposes of God for the Adamic white race and the world. It would be preposterous to think that God would even consider Cain's offering: "God accepted the offering from Abel, but rejected the offering of Cain because he was unworthy, that is, he was of the serpent."[20]

After Cain's offering is rejected, he entices Abel to "go out to the field" with him, and there he kills him (Gen. 4:8). As Satan's offspring, Cain has the natural inclination to be a murderer. This act of Cain is taken to be the beginning of the "enmity" between the races spoken of in Genesis 3:15, "the first overt expression of the enmity or hatred" between the seed of the serpent and the seed of Adam. After killing Abel, Cain acts true to his nature as Satan's kid and lies about his heinous act. When God asks where Abel is, Cain answers, "I do not know; am I my brother's keeper?" (Gen. 4:9). Murder and lies are also parts of the racial urge of the present-day Jew, Identity adherents contend.

Through Identity's interpretation of Genesis 4 and the role of Cain, certain questions are brought to the text and answered. One such question is where Cain might have obtained a wife if Adam and Eve were the first human beings created by God. "If there were no other peoples on the earth who was Cain afraid of? . . . Cain was cast out, who did he marry if there were no other people?"[21] The Identity answer is that Adam and Eve were not the first people created; there were pre-Adamic people of color whose existence outside the Aryan cradle answers the questions regarding Cain's wife and associations. Cain "went away from the presence of God, and settled in the land of Nod, east of Eden" (Gen. 4:16), and in Nod, Identity adherents claim, he intermarried with the pre-Adamic people of color. And because of his superior, albeit satanic origins, Cain became a great leader among the pre-Adamites. He was the source of idol and devil worship, decadent secular civilization, and through his seed-line, all that is opposed to God. Cain comes to loom over Identity theology and history in ways that far outweigh his actual role in the Genesis narratives and the Bible as a whole. Selections from Identity material corroborate these Cainite interpretations:

> We believe that the Adam-man of Genesis was the placing of the White race upon this earth. Not all races descend from Adam. Adam is the father of the White race only. . . . We believe that there are literal children of Satan in the world today. These children are the descendants of Cain, who was a result of Eve's original sin, her physical seduction by Satan. We know that because of this sin there is a battle and a natural enmity between the children of Satan and the children of The Most High God.[22]

> We believe the White, Anglo-Saxon, Germanic and kindred people to be God's true, literal Children of Israel. Only this race fulfills every detail of Biblical Prophecy and World History concerning Israel. . . . We believe in an existing be-

ing known as the Devil or Satan and called the Serpent, who has literal "seed" or posterity in the earth commonly called Jews today.[23]

THE FLOOD: PUNISHMENT FOR RACE MIXING

Interpretation of the Bible in racial terms continues with the narrative of Noah and the Flood (Gen. 6:1–8:22). Identity adherents claim that the Flood was geographically localized, a punishment by God inflicted on the Adamic race, not for general wickedness but for the specific sin of race mixing. Using unsubstantiated historical information including a long-standing myth concerning the origins of the Aryan race, Identity adherents believe that the Adamic race was created in a mountain-ringed basin in present-day central China. While the pre-Adamic "beasts of the field" roamed the lowlands outside the mountain-ringed basin, God's chosen white race was placed in a cradle to preserve racial integrity and spiritual stature.

Seclusion was not total, however, and Identity adherents use brief biblical references to legendary supernatural "sons of God" and "daughters of humans" during a pre-Flood period to assert that Adamic white males were guilty of venturing out of the God-given cradle and race mixing with pre-Adamic women (Gen. 6:2, 4). At first only a few Adamites ventured out, they claim, but eventually many more wives were chosen from pre-Adamic races. Because of the sin of race mixing and the threat posed to the spiritual stature of the Adamic race, God punished the Adamic race by flooding the mountain-ringed basin. But because of God's covenant with Adam, and because Noah was "a thoroughbred, not a mongrel," God permitted a remnant, Noah and his family, to survive. Upon receiving instruction from God and being "a survivalist," Noah built the ark and preserved the Adamic race. [24]

There are some variations to these formulations, but what is held in common is a consistently racial interpretation of the Flood. Some claim that God punished the pre-Adamites because of the increasing and alluring danger of race mixing.

Others claim that the "sons of God" were sinister beings that possessed Adamic men and coerced them into taking wives from among the pre-Adamites. And still others claim that the Flood was universal, that quite literally "waters swelled so mightily on the earth that all the high mountains under the whole heaven were covered" (Gen. 7:19). Yet in this scenario, in keeping with the promise of enmity given in Genesis 3:15, Cain's seed must have survived the Flood by entering the ark among the pairs of "all flesh" (Gen. 6:19–20). When Noah boarded the ark, the "seed of the serpent" entered as "unclean flesh": "The Seed . . . survived the flood. . . . [They] are not, of course, Adamic Seed and therefore were not counted among Noah and his family or as 'people.'"[25]

This racial interpretation of Genesis is the lens through which Identity reads the rest of the Bible and sees all of faith and life. Religious racists are often accused of pulling one or two verses out of the Bible and basing their whole worldview on them, but this is not really the case with Identity theology. Although these racial extremists do read certain verses out of context, they interpret and operate from a center. They have a hermeneutic, a lens through which to read the Scriptures. And based on this hermeneutic, their interpretation has some coherence. . . . Who is left that thinks the end of the aberration of racism that blossomed in the 1930s and 1940s has finally been reached? The ideology, indeed the theology, of modern racism has developed and gone further in its incorporation of the pieces and people of the Bible and of our world.

NOTES

1. Skurdal, Common Law Edict, 3; see also *Censored Bible Teachings* (Lynchburg, Va.: Virginia Publishing Company, n.d.).

2. Personal correspondence from Dan Gayman, December 14, 1995.

3. $100 Billion Freemen Lien against Pastor Jerry Walters, 9. Based on its use in chapters 5 and 9 of Genesis, the Freemen would need to change their interpretation of the word *image* (shadow, dark color), otherwise Seth would be black; this would be anathema for them: "[Adam] became the father of a son in his likeness, according to his *image,* and named him Seth" (Gen. 5:3).

This is also true of the pronouncement after the Flood, when it is asserted that all the survivors are made in God's image: "in his own image God made humankind" (Gen. 9:6).

4. *Articles of Faith and Doctrine,* 8; *Kingdom Identity Ministries Doctrinal Statement of Beliefs* (Harrison, Ark.: Kingdom Identity Ministries, n.d.), 5.

5. Bertrand Comparet, *Your Heritage: An Identification of the True Israel through Biblical and Historical Sources* (Harrison, Ark.: Kingdom Identity Ministries, n.d.), 3, 36.

6. Sheldon Emry, *Heirs of the Promise: Abraham's Children* (Sandpoint, Idaho: America's Promise Ministries, n.d.), 25; J.H. Allen, *Judah's Sceptre and Joseph's Birthright* (Merrimac, Mass.: Destiny Publishers, 1917), 79.

7. *Doctrinal Statement of Beliefs,* 7; *Noah's Flood Was Not World-Wide* (Harrison, Ark.: Kingdom Identity Ministries, n.d.).

8. *$100 Billion Freemen Lien,* 6. See also *Doctrinal Statement of Beliefs,* 8-9; Gentry, *Death Penalty,* 2. In contrast to Identity's interpretation, the Hebrew wordplay between *adam* (man) and *adamah* (ground) emphasizes creatureliness, connection to the ground, and utter dependence on God. When God withdraws God's breath, man dies. Man is created from the earth (Gen. 2:7), must work the soil (3:23), and then returns to the earth when he dies (3:19). *Adam,* which can include reference to *ruddy, reddened,* or *to be red,* does not refer to the rose-red cheeks of a white Adam or to superiority, but points to the ground, the reddish brown earth *(adamah)* that Adam's complexion resembles, from which Adam came, and to which Adam will return. Humankind is made in the image of God, but made of dust as well. Adam is an earthling from the earth, a human from the humus.

9. Dan Gayman, *The Two Seeds of Genesis 3:15,* rev. ed. (Shell City, Mass.: Church of Israel, 1994), 192.

10. *Doctrinal Statement of Beliefs,* 6.

11. Gayman, *Two Seeds,* 210.

12. Ibid., 67.

13. Saxon, *The Mask of Edom,* 22.

14. *Freeman Edict,* 3; see also David Lane, *Under This Sign You Shall Conquer: Identity* (Hayden Lake, Idaho: Aryan Nations, n.d.), 3-4. This pamphlet was written by David Lane of the Order, a group responsible for a string of western crimes in 1984. Lane, who was convicted of driving the getaway vehicle after the 1984 murder of Alan Berg, a Jewish radio talk-show host from Denver, believes he is a prisoner of war held by the Zionist Occupation Government.

15. Four hours of taped lectures by James Wickstrom, Posse Comitatus.

16. Gayman, *Two Seeds,* 23; Neser, *The Serpent of Genesis 3; Articles of Faith and Doctrine,* 9-10.

17. Gayman, *Two Seeds,* 80.

18. Ibid., 121.

19. *$100 Billion Freemen Lien,* 7; *In the Image of God,* 33.

20. Eustace Mullins, *The Curse of Canaan* (n.p.: Sons of Liberty, n.d.), 35. Jack Mohr, *Birthright or the Right to Govern* (St. Louis: n.p., n.d.), 2.

21. *$100 Billion Lien*, 8.

22. *Yesterday: The Tribes of Israel, Today: The White Christian Nations* (Hayden Lake, Idaho: Aryan Nations, n.d.).

23. *Doctrinal Statement of Beliefs*, 5–6.

24. *Noah's Flood Was Not World-Wide;* Pete Peters, *The Bible: Handbook for Survivalists, Racists, Tax Protesters, Militants and Right-Wing Extremists* (Laporte, Colo.: Scriptures for America, n.d.), 5; Bob Hallstrom, *The Law of Segregation* (Boise: Gospel Ministries, n.d.), part 1.

25. Gayman, *Two Seeds*, 222, 227.

White Separatist Ideology

BETTY A. DOBRATZ AND STEPHANIE L. SHANKS-MEILE

The following selection by Betty A. Dobratz and Stephanie L. Shanks-Meile defines today's white power movement as separatist rather than "supremacist" in orientation. Many white power advocates want to establish both genetic and territorial separation from other races and claim no desire to dominate or destroy other racial and cultural groups. Some white nationalists also reject the concepts of equality and liberalism, maintaining that a dictatorial or aristocratic government would best serve the needs of a future white racial state. Some segments of the white separatist movement have been willing to work with separatists of other ethnicities to bring about an eventual division of the races, the authors report. Dobratz and Shanks-Meile are the authors of *"White Power, White Pride!": The White Separatist Movement in the United States.*

M any social scientists have viewed the white supremacist movement as a reactionary movement that wants to re-create a past social order. Somewhat similarly, the movement has been viewed as a countermovement to defeat or destroy the already existing civil rights movement. However, we believe that much of today's movement is separatist in orientation, wanting to remove its supporters from an integrated society. According to William E. Barker, a former law enforcement officer who wrote a book describing the recent movement especially in the Northwest, "Although it cannot be denied that racist and supremacist beliefs are embraced by many in the movement, the term separatist probably goes further in defining their position than does supremacist. To them,

Excerpted from *"White Power, White Pride!": The White Separatist Movement in the United States,* by Betty A. Dobratz and Stephanie L. Shanks-Meile (New York: Twayne, 1997). Copyright © 1997 by Twayne Publishers. Reprinted with permission.

THE LATE TWENTIETH CENTURY • 157

the issue of racial separation is inherently more important than the desire for racial dominance or control."

Mrs. David (Katja) Lane of Wotansvolk—14 Word Press suggested that white separatism was key, whereas white supremacy wasn't significant:

> Most white people that I know inside and outside the movement don't want to run anybody else's life, do not want to dominate other people, other nations. . . . I know personally in my heart I don't want to own or run China, or Africa, or Latin America or any other race or continent. And I don't think most people in the white power movement do. We just need to find our own place on this planet and we have come to recognize that it's an absolute requirement if we're going to survive, and we're denied our own nation, our own schools, neighborhoods, organizations, everything necessary for racial survival. To talk about whether one race is supreme is really irrelevant.

She also believed that the label *supremacist* could be used to demonize those in the movement.

THE SEPARATIST AGENDA

The closeness of the 1995 vote over a secessionist referendum in Quebec Canada and the events in the former Yugoslavia are only two cases that illustrate the significance of the separatist agenda. According to sociologist James Davis, "separatism reflects the belief that the only possible and acceptable route open to the group is total withdrawal from the dominant community." In the United States it was probably whites who first suggested separatist solutions to white and black relations in the eighteenth century.

Tamotsu Shibutani and Kuan M. Kwan considered separatism as part of the struggle for cultural pluralism and indicated that separatists tend to do the following:

1. "Conceive of themselves as a group apart, a separate entity, not as a part of a larger population."
2. Believe that their values are the only ones of real sig-

nificance. They are not apologetic about their beliefs or customs.
3. Criticize others who do not support them, using terms such as deserters.
4. Emphasize the significance of ancestry or biological lineage, thus condemning intermarriage.
5. Reinforce their in-group feelings through rituals and celebrations of days of ideological significance.
6. Display their symbols with great pride, although many in society see them as marks of shame. Instead of feeling humiliation, they resent society for their condemnations.
7. Stress the glorious past.

In addition, Shibutani and Kwan noted that some may be "ardent racists" and their ideology may be supported by the complementary sentiments of love of the in-group and hatred toward the out-group.

Since separatism involves withdrawal from contact with the dominant community, one may wonder why some whites would be advocating separatism for themselves when they are considered part of the dominant group. However, most whites in this movement do not see themselves as part of the dominant group and indeed feel betrayed by other whites who characterize them as racists and troublemakers. The music band Blue Eyed Devils makes this clear in the chorus of their song "Walk in Shame":

Nigger lover, race traitor
Walk in shame and hide your face
Nigger lover, race traitor
For false pride you sold out your race
So now it's a civil war, white against white
You against me, and I'll take your life

The predicted future race war will not likely be strictly black against white.

Michael Barkun discusses territorial separation in the movement and points out that while the white separatists may disagree on certain parts, "all agree that short of overthrowing

ZOG [the Zionist Occupational Government], the best path for the racialist right lies in somehow carving out a separate state." Mostly the area conceived of for the homeland is the Pacific Northwest within the borders of Washington, Oregon, Idaho, Montana, and Wyoming; this has been referred to as the Northwest Imperative. However, when Richard Butler of Aryan Nations (AN) originally discussed a homeland as early as 1980, he seems to have envisioned something like John Harrell's "Golden Triangle." Christian-Patriots Defense League's Harrell had extolled people to withdraw to the center of the continent (the Midwest) to wait out evil Communism. Barkun believes the original suggestion of the Pacific Northwest probably came from Bob Miles in 1982. James Aho suggests that Donald Clerkin of the Euro-American Alliance may have first advanced the idea of an "Europolis" as an armed encampment to be established in rough terrain, hard to access for those unwelcomed. Butler then reissued Clerkin's call. According to Major Clerkin in his March 13, 1996, letter to us, the late Pastor Bob Miles first told him about territorial separation of Aryans in North America. Since Clerkin is a Europeanist, he used the name "Europolis" for the proposed Aryan homeland.

In an undated publication entitled *The Birth of a Nation: A Declaration of the Existence of a Racial Nation Within Confines of a Hostile Political State,* Miles argued that the white race was at a crucial juncture because the political state was trying to destroy all racial differences:

> The course of the political state departs from the original beliefs of our fathers and the founders of this national State. *It is not the racial Nation which secedes from the political State. It is the political State which has seceded from the beliefs and the principles of our originally combined State and Nation. They have left us!*

Miles was thus putting the responsibility on the federal government for possible secession. He rejected armed rebellion and implored the political state to leave white separatists like himself alone:

> *If we are the modern "Neanderthals", then leave us in peace! Let*

us, our families, and our children be free of your modernistic garbage, your cookie-mold laws designed to compress everyone into a mud-colored nothingness! Let us go in peace! Let us be considered a Racial Nation of Aryans, living within the man-made boundaries of a political State. Let us be recognized as a Folk who have different beliefs, values, and different life-styles than those which comprise your "loyal" citizenry. Accept us as an element which is dolefully indigestible to you. You cannot consume us. You cannot absorb us. We are a strain that you cannot eliminate.

Miles included a map that was entitled "The Re-ethnization of North America," which illustrates the "alien invasion of North America" depicting territories of "mainly White Aryan occupation," "expanding alien, non-white occupation," and "heavy concentration of non-whites forces." The white areas were mainly in the five northwest states but included parts of Nevada, Utah, and Colorado.

According to *WAR* Miles indicated at the 1986 AN Congress that the Northwest Territorial Imperative would be achieved:

by White racialists moving to the area, buying land together or adjacent to each other and having families consisting of five and ten children. These children would be raised and educated in the tradition and fighting heritage of our own White people. We will win the Northwest by out-breeding our opponents and keeping our children away from the insane and destructive values of the Establishment.

Miles used religious justifications for the Aryan state by maintaining that Aryan spirituality should be free from contamination.

THE RACIAL STATE

Aryan Nations blends the concepts of race, religion, and politics/nation together to provide a form of unity in which race and religion neatly coincide under one national boundary. "Aryan Nations Theopolitical Platform" calls "for the re-establishment of White Aryan sovereignty over the lands of

Aryan settlement and occupation" and "our Race is our Nation on earth." Further, according to the "Platform for the Aryan National State," only Aryans are allowed citizenship in this nation state, including voting rights, owning property, serving in the military or in law enforcement, holding political office, and so on. (Article I). True positive Christianity is encouraged, and other religious practices such as Talmudism (Judaism) and devil and heathen religions should be stopped (Article IV). Jews would be repatriated and their wealth redistributed. All members of the media would have to be citizens; publishing and circulating material not in the national welfare would be forbidden.

Many others connect the racial state with racial survival. A prominent movement figure, Louis Beam, argued: "We must now separate ourselves from the mongrel nation that envelopes us. If our race is to have a future then a nation for ourselves, of ourselves, and by ourselves must be born on this continent!" David Lane, in "White Genocide Manifesto," demanded "exclusive White homelands" in both Europe and North America because "the highest law is the preservation of one's kind." The *NSV Report,* a quarterly journal of the National Socialist Vanguard, published "Brief History of the White Nationalist Movement," which described the movement as supporting a territorial imperative for a white nation and complete geographic separation of the world's races. The article suggested Klan groups did not press for geographic separation after World War II but over time have become more favorably disposed to this kind of separatism; the National Socialist and Christian Identity groups have always been white nationalist in orientation.

REJECTING EQUALITY

In his essay "The Coming Aryan Republic," Donald Clerkin argued that the "multi-racial/multi-cultural Staat" of "Washington criminal mongrelizers" could not be maintained. Instead of drawing very much on the U.S. Constitution, he recommended a system like the Roman Republic:

All that is salvageable from that document [the Constitution] is certain elements of the Bill of Rights. The Constitution is therefore a tainted form, especially in the idea that *equality* should be the cornerstone of a government that serves the Aryan people. WE therefore totally reject the concept of not only racial equality, but also the false notion of individual equality. We have seen how unequally endowed individuals are in this world. Friedrich Nietzsche rightly stated that equality in nature is a fiction held by ideological fools and dangerous social tinkerers.

What we have designed to govern us is removed to the period of the Roman Republic. The period of Roman Republicanism, which lasted four hundred years (circa 450 B.C. to 50 B.C.), is the most perfect example of an aristocratic governance, one that reflected the innate inequality of individuals. Face it, most U.S. citizens do not vote; they don't care how they are governed. Media tell them what to think on a day-to-day basis. . . .

The Roman Republic was based upon the solidarity of the family as the prime unit in society. . . .

We Aryans must reject the concept of equality—absolutely, as we construct our new Republic. This is not to say that the Aryan Republic will mistreat its people. Were it to descend to that level of misconduct, it would not be tolerated. But there is a natural "pecking order" in human affairs, just as there is amongst the lower orders of mammals. We cannot ignore this rank structure and succeed. Again, those who cannot stomach the idea that all men are definitely NOT created equal; they must resign themselves to the old, corrupt system operated by the Washington criminals. Our Aryan Republic will not tolerate liberalism. . . .

This Aryan Republic will be representative in operation. . . . Each person in the Aryan Republic will know his place—and be respected for serving in his place.

James Mason in *Siege* advocated Hitler's National Socialism for the "state-to-be" once the system was destroyed. Rather than supporting authority at the county level, as Posse Comitatus had done, . . . Mason argued for a strong centralized dictatorship:

> In our view, the function of government is as the leader of its people, not merely caretaker or arbiter. Hitler said that the leading forces make the society and nation what it is and what it will become. This means taking the youth firmly in hand raising them up in the manner that our ideology commands so as to achieve the ever-more-perfect Race and State in the shortest possible time. Only a centralized government can accomplish this. So-called "rights" and "freedom" all take distant back seats to this highest goal. The task must be accomplished without petty interference from any quarter. . . . The word that will sooner or later pop up is dictatorship. We favor dictatorship: our own.

Mason is clear about what he perceives to be the best form of indoctrination and socialization in the separatist state.

A NATURAL ARISTOCRACY

"W.A.R. Position Paper *America First or Race First*" suggests that WAR and Tom Metzger may have been the first to actually name the "ideological struggle as White Separatism." Metzger does not object to the Northwest Imperative but argues that the idea would not be "practical until after some kind of confrontation with the system. The system would never let you peacefully amass in one center of the country to promote ideas with which they do not agree." Other concerns of his revolve around economic issues and the amount of commitment to separatism:

> There is not an abundance of work in the Pacific Northwest. You have to have capital. You have to have people to come in and run the companies in which your people will work. You can do it, but it has to be based on somewhat of a fanatical zeal, and in the meetings I have been to on this, I just have not heard or see [sic] that zeal. I have heard talk.

In our interview, Metzger touched on his conception of the Aryan nation-state, which was quite Social Darwinist. In the spirit of Robert Michels's "iron law of oligarchy," Metzger indicated: "We believe that there is an aristocracy, a natural aristocracy that will rise to the top of any society, . . . an honest and good aristocracy . . . looking after the best interest of the culture and the race." He also indicated there shouldn't be any class barriers so that through competition whites from various social classes could become leaders. The emphasis would be on "the blood and the brains," suggesting that one's racial heritage and intelligence would be important in determining who would be the leaders. WAR also recommends applying white separatism internationally, pointing out the arbitrariness of national borders, and advocates smaller racial states that would be less likely to be drawn into the arms race and would be more aware of limited amounts of resources.

Somewhat similar to Metzger's view is Wilmot Robertson's conception of the "ethnostate" that would be created through "separation and reduction into small-scale political units, not accelerated coagulation into ever larger nations, empires and spheres of interest." The foreword to his book *The Ethnostate* identifies the significance of race to this new formulation:

> What is called for is a new form of government that would transform socially destructive into socially constructive forces. Race, now actively tearing countries apart, might be helpful in putting them back together, but this time in the form of autonomous, relatively self-sufficient collectivities that the author has chosen to designate as ethnostates.

Wilmot Robertson stresses that the "basic *sine qua non* of an ethnostate, the prop on which it succeeds or fails, is racial and cultural homogeneity" but that being small in terms of both territory and population is essential as well. The ethnostate offers a sense of identity for its citizens and "is perhaps the only peaceful and sensible means of assuring white survival in an increasingly antiwhite, nonwhite world."

The National Office of the National Alliance in its pamphlet *What Is the National Alliance?* called for white living space and an Aryan society that would be "racially clean." It includes an international design in which the white world would be rooted in Aryan values and harmonious with Aryan nature. This world would not necessarily be homogeneous, for there could be different societies such as Germanic, Slavic, Celtic, and so on.

SEPARATION VERSUS SEGREGATION

Separatism rather than *segregation* is used by most movement people to describe their position. The International Separatist Front (ISF) defines the two concepts as:

> SEGREGATION: Socially enforced isolation of a race, class, or ethnic group backed by a system of law. Always results in discrimination and lack of redress and opportunity for the oppressed group. Segregation eventually leads to rebellion by the segregated group.
>
> SEPARATION: The maintenance of very separate and distinct cultures by divisions drawn primarily along racial and geographical lines. The desire and opportunity for self-determination. Free choice to remain with one's own kind in a setting free from unwanted intrusion by other racial groups, their influences, their political, and their religious systems. Freedom from oppressive genocidal governments. Racial sovereignty.

In our interview with him, Dennis Mahon, who is affiliated with WAR, expressed his dissatisfaction with segregation as "having the Blacks live on one side of the tracks and at night they go back there but during the day they're mowing your lawn—that's segregation. No, that's hypocritical as hell. . . . We got to do our own dirty work." James Dillavou of AN did not advocate segregation as a final goal of the movement, but he did see it as an acceptable short-term possibility before the beginning of separation in the United States. "If it was law and legal to do—have a white school and a black school—fine. I'd have no problem with it. . . . As the end desired thing—no, we

would not want a segregationist society. But today's society. . . .
It's a first basic step. . . . It depends on the situation."

Matt Hale, leader of National Socialist White Americans
Party when interviewed and now leader of the World Church
of the Creator, suggested crucial distinctions between the
views of the past and the present:

> We are separatists. We are—we don't consider ourselves su-
> premacists in a sense because we are not out to rule anyone.
> We do believe the white race is a superior race, but we're not
> looking for the old, white supremacy where the white man's
> on top, the black man's on bottom and the black man is
> working for the white man, etc. We'd like to have a total ge-
> ographical separation where no race is oppressing the other.

Jeff Schoep, a young man of the National Socialist American
Workers Freedom Movement, also indicated to us his support
of this view:

> Well, we believe that the white people should have their
> own territorial imperative, their own nation. As in all the
> other races. National self-determination for all people. We
> agree with that so the blacks and everyone else deserves
> their own country also. We're not by any means out for the
> extermination of any race. We believe that everyone de-
> serves their own country.

John C. Sigler III, aka "Duck," of Confederate Hammer Skinheads points out the applicability of separatism to the movement's goals:

> To me, the term white separatism is simply a statement of
> our objectives. Any rational person must accept the fact that
> other races and cultures are not going to simply disappear,
> therefore, in order to continue our own cultural and per-
> haps genetic evolution, separatism represents the best inter-
> ests of our people.

While most of our respondents view separatism positively,
Molly Gill, who publishes *The Radical Feminist,* felt white separatism "means we whites will congregate in some living area

such as the Northwest but it is a cop-out and sell-out since we Aryans founded and developed this USA as it was before the rot of the sixties was promoted by the Jews." She quite clearly sees the Northwest Imperative as an overly restrictive solution.

Not everyone in the movement makes clear-cut distinctions between separatism and segregation though. For example, in our interview with Rodney Stubbs, the Imperial Wizard of the American KKKK in Indiana, he felt the meaning of white separatism was similar to segregation and commented:

> I believe segregation—the blacks should stay with the blacks, the whites with the whites. . . . Like the forced integration of schools and busing—I'm totally against that—you know. Working—at the workplace—ah, I see no problem with whites being able to work with blacks at a steel mill or wherever—but when they go home at night, the white goes home to his white family and the black should go home to his black or the gook or whoever we're talking about.

Even within the social science literature, the distinction may not always be clear between segregation and separatism. Thomas Pettigrew, in his book *Racially Separate or Together,* did not seem to distinguish between segregation and separatism. He identified three key ideological assumptions of white separatists that have parallels for black separatists:

1. "Whites and Negroes are more comfortable apart than together."
2. "Negroes are inherently inferior to whites, and this is the underlying reality of all racial problems."
3. "Since contact can never be mutually beneficial, it will inevitably lead to racial conflict."

Pettigrew included the belief in white superiority in his assumptions of white separatism, but, as we have seen, movement members would not necessarily agree with this.

WHITE SEPARATIST ALLIES

Many in the mainstream may find the Eastern Hammer Skinheads white separatist definition of the Nation of Islam surprising. It is "the greatest ally of the White Separatist movement, who work for the logical end to an age of quarrel." Since the Nation of Islam and white separatists both favor the separation of the races, some in the movement advocate working together to achieve this goal. In a few cases the belief in separatism has actually prompted leaders of certain groups to work with blacks who favor separatism. Tom Metzger, for example, met with Black Panthers and even made a donation to Farrakhan. He told us that although Farrakhan was a fantastic speaker, he was concerned about separatists who use religious appeals. He commented: "I don't trust preachers and it seems like every time I try to deal with somebody who's a minister or preacher, I end up having problems. After working for over 10 years at building some kind of consensus and negotiations with blacks, we've come to the conclusion that we don't think it's going to happen." He felt that the black leaders weren't able to develop an infrastructure that would result in serious regional discussions.

According to *The Klansman* article "Unlikely Alliance Black Activists and Klan Unite against the System," members of The Invisible Empire, KKKK of Florida had joint demonstrations with black national activists who belonged to the Pan-African Inter-National Movement (PAIN) led by Chief Elder Osiris Akkebala. At one particular meeting, Akkebala maintained that racism involves the power to oppress, but the Klan today doesn't have such power and therefore is not a racist organization. John Baumgardner, then Grand Dragon of the Florida Klan, told the crowd that he favored repatriations and a reparation proposal made by PAIN. Having these joint meetings evidently led to some dissent among members of the national Klan, which may have been one of the reasons Baumgardner left that Klan. According to our interview with him:

> We held a number of joint demonstrations here in Florida
> in the year before I left the Klan, which initially met with
> a lot of support from Klan leadership because I guess they
> thought that was an idea that could be exploited. We didn't
> look at it that way. We had developed a relationship with

these people over a period of about six years and worked closer and closer with them behind the scenes and finally decided that we needed to take it out into the public's view and show them that maybe some of their ideas about the Klan weren't exactly correct. That we were able and willing to work with other races on issues that we shared a viewpoint in common. And, while it was popular at first with the national leadership, I think that overall the Klan membership around the country did not support the idea and put a lot of pressure on the national leadership to reject that and that's eventually what they did. They rejected the program. . . .

The June 1996 edition of the *Florida Interklan Report* edited by Baumgardner reported that he and a fellow Klansman had recently attended a Pan-African gathering in Orlando in which Minister Khalid Abdul Muhammed of the Nation of Islam identified the white man as "the Devil." Another part of that *Florida Interklan Report* explained why it is important to work with other racial separatists:

Separation is the only answer for our problems—everything else has been tried. . . . Some militant blacks talk about how many crackers they are going to kill. I say kill all the crackers you want but leave white separatists alone or we will kill you. We know how to do that too. What we are trying to do by working with other racial separatists is prevent wholesale bloodshed. Some blood will obviously have to be spilled to get the government off our backs and to get the die-hard ignorant reactionaries out of the way but until that happens nothing substantial is going to change for the better.

Although certainly not typical, these are examples where parts of the movement have been willing to work with others of a different race who share the same strategy of racial separation. For movement members, racial separation should ideally lead to the movement achieving the preservation of the race.

America First or Race First?

WHITE ARYAN RESISTANCE

The following selection—originally a web article posted by White Aryan Resistance (WAR)—defines the concept of white separatism and distinguishes it from white supremacy or white nationalism. The unnamed author argues that the term "supremacist" is a media label given to separatists who wish to cultivate allegiances based on race rather than nation. White separatists do not subscribe to patriotic nationalism, the author points out, because the idea of "nation" too often includes people of different races and cultures.

White Aryan Resistance (W.A.R.) and Tom Metzger were probably the first to coin our ideological struggle as White Separatism. Even though our economic determinist enemies continue to simplistically label us as White Supremacists, our message is slowly getting through. There surely are White Elitist Supremacists, however they operate in the economic determinist camp, [who pretend] to fight "naughty" racism (belief in one's own race).

From the breakaway republics in the Soviet Union, to the Northern Indian colony of Kashmir—or even closer, Quebec in Canada—ethnicity and culture are again gaining their proper place on the world stage.

HOW THE WHITE RACE BECAME ENSLAVED

Extremists on the Left rail against the reemergence of Nationalism, while [those in] the Right Wing rail for America first. The Left continues to support the idea of suppression of nationalistic moves, preferring the failed "bigger is better" attitude of the last several decades. The so-called Right has correctly argued against a world class Universalist Cult, while at the same time supporting an equally dangerous transnational economic program which falsely equates Capitalism with Free Enterprise. When discussing the Right and the Left however, things can become very confusing. The majority of the Right has followed the lead of the Left, into programs and laws, suppressing discrimination. Discrimination and property ownership are the two issues that separate all mankind from slavery. Without the ability to discriminate, ethnic and racial protection is impossible. Anyone who advocates laws against discrimination or private ownership of property becomes your enemy, no matter what racial group they belong to, or which flag they happen to wave.

One must remember that forced integration and the outlawing of discrimination increased at the same rate as state control of private property. These anti-Separatist ideas were enacted under the various flags of the so-called Democracies. Under Old Glory and the Pledge of Allegiance, our race became enslaved.

SEPARATISTS ARE NOT NATIONALISTS

Remember those anti-Separatist words "... one nation indivisible, with liberty and justice for all ..." Separatists are not Nationalists. For the most part, a Separatist sees national borders as lines drawn arbitrarily, to the tune of economic guidance, not for racial or cultural best interests.

For today, what is this nation? It is certainly no longer an identifiable, homogeneous, racial or cultural group. What, in some cases, may have had its beginnings as race and culture, today is simply an economic outline that encloses any combination of races and beliefs. This, of course, is not a real nation. This is a bastard nation, with almost no roots, where millions of non-Whites can claim only one generation on the land. That land usually being the asphalted big metropolis. These sad places cannot, without tongue in cheek, be called cities or city-states. They are like overnight mining camps, that rise in population, until they suck out the environmental resources and then collapse. The metropolises are the gaping anal cavities of a sick and dying nation. To those unclean places flock the worst of all races. Only the most degenerate of the White race struggle to stay on top of the maggot pile in such unnatural settings.

In the face of these twin monstrosities lie the bastardized metropolis of *Blade Runner* fame and the artificial rainbow nation. Separatist movements, world wide, are truly a renaissance of natural logic.

The drastic differences between a real racist, which is a White Separatist, and a White Nationalist of today, are very important. To a White Separatist, the overriding importance is race, not what we have known as nation, in this [twentieth] century. The White Separatist, by his or her very nature, must applaud racial and cultural Separatism worldwide.

Your masters do not fear you as an Economic Separatist, however they do fear you as a true Racial Separatist. If the Soviet Republics have the ethnic and cultural right of self-determination, why do not the states of the United States? When the economic determinists applaud the various Separatist moves in other areas of the world, why not in North America?

AN ADVANCE TO STATE SOVEREIGNTY

Some would say that this is a return to states rights, while in fact it is an advance to state sovereignty. There should follow a competition of the states. The states or regions that are convinced that their future is best protected by the advancement of the black race should openly advertise that fact. Those states or regions that desire a homogeneous Euro-American or White population should advertise as such. Those states or regions that believe that the Mexican and Central American population would provide the future with the most healthy environment should advertise as such. In other words, total freedom of choice. We hear a lot about freedom of choice lately, don't we? When was the last time you heard of freedom of choice on the subject of race or racial separation?

The press has, in the last twelve years, for the most part frozen out any portion of an interview that outlined or even mentioned the idea of Separatism. No matter what you label yourself as, the press always uses the terms, "White Supremacist" or "Neo-Nazi." These terms are then predigested, as to what Pavlov's sheep are in turn supposed to say and do, in reaction to those few brave enough to even mention the possibility of Separatism.

Miscegenation: The Campaign to Destroy the White Race

WILLIAM PIERCE

William Pierce, a former member of the American Nazi Party, is the leader of the National Alliance, a white separatist group that sprang up in the late 1960s. In the following essay, Pierce contends that the recent increase in miscegenation or "race-mixing" is the result of a Jewish-controlled media campaign to slowly destroy the white race. The news and entertainment industry, he claims, makes whites feel guilty for being white and promotes the message that mating with nonwhites and having nonwhite children is the trendy and morally correct thing to do. Despite this propaganda, Pierce maintains, most whites do not participate in race-mixing and the continuing attempts to encourage miscegenation will fail if confronted by organized and radical separatist activism.

H istory has taught us that the most fundamental necessities for the existence of a healthy and progressive White society are the racial quality of its members and a moral code or value system which complements and enhances that quality.

Ultimately, of course, the former is much more fundamental than the latter. Only a sound race can give birth to sound racial ethics. Without the living biological entity, there is and can be nothing. But as long as the race survives—as long as the potential for effective racial sovereignty exists—alien and spiritually damaging values alone will not prove fatal.

The enemies of our race have obviously long understood this truth. That is why, a half-century ago, they waged the most vicious war the world has ever seen in order to destroy an idea based upon that racial truth. That is why they subsequently organized the systematic swamping of White civilization by millions of alien immigrants. And that is why they have used their control of the news and entertainment media, of the government, and of schools and universities to implement a massive propaganda campaign to encourage miscegenation between Whites and non-Whites.

MISCEGENATION IS NOT NATURAL

Of course, miscegenation is not a natural occurrence. Evolution would have been impossible if every evolutionary experiment had been short-circuited by cross-breeding. Nature's urge toward higher and more complex life forms has demanded that subspecies remain genetically isolated until all possibility of genetic admixture has been removed. Even though such isolation of the various human subspecies from one another has not been of sufficient length to ensure the impossibility of genetic admixture, it has ensured the existence of deep-seated psychological barriers which, under natural conditions, prevent miscegenation.

When these natural conditions are disrupted and distorted, however, unnatural sexual activities such as homosexuality and miscegenation have been known to result. Just as bulls have been known to mount mares, and St. Bernard dogs have tried to mate with Chihuahuas when forced into close confinement and deprived of their natural environment, so Whites have copulated with Negroes in similar circumstances. It is the disruption of the White man's natural environment and the dehumanization of his society and culture, therefore, which the Jews and their collaborators in the news and entertainment media have consistently worked for in order to encourage racial mixing. This campaign began at least as early as 1967, when 16 U.S. states still had laws against miscegenation. In that year Jewish director/producer Stanley Kramer brought out the film *Guess Who's Coming to Dinner*, starring Katherine Hepburn and Spencer Tracy as a couple whose daughter begins an affair with a Negro. The aim of the film was clear and since has been admitted. It was designed as an "educational film" for White Americans: after seeing their on-screen heroes, Tracy and Hepburn, surrendering their White daughter to a Black male, they would feel less compunction in doing the same.[1]

Since that time Whites have not just been encouraged to mate with Blacks, Hispanics, and Asians, they have been subject to every conceivable Pavlovian method to blackmail and bully them emotionally into doing so. With ever increasing intensity the message has been that miscegenation is not just an option, but the option that society expects. Particularly, the primary aim of the Political Correctness movement, in all of its manifestations, has been to confuse heterosexual Whites and make them feel sinful and guilty for being White; to encourage them to "repent" by helping put their race out of existence.

PERNICIOUS RACE-MIXING PROPAGANDA

The Hollywood film *Last of the Mohicans,* which came out in 1992 with the Jewish actor Daniel Day-Lewis in the leading role, is a typical example of how the Jewish news and entertainment media have spearheaded this campaign. In the film White males are portrayed as weak, cowardly, disloyal, and barbaric—and as justly deserving of their slaughter at the hands of the noble, dignified, courageous, and sexy Red Indians. Yes, just to ensure that White women don't miss the implication that White men are worthless, the leading White female character dumps her despicable British-officer fiancé and runs off into the sunset with the Mohican hero. The underlying message of the film is clear: race-mixing is not only natural and understandable, it is also the morally right thing to do.

Zoologists and anthropologists have identified two types of feral constraint which ensure that under natural conditions animal groups—including human groups—may be able to interbreed with each other or refrain from doing so. On one hand, there are inborn biological impulses based upon physical "sign stimuli," such as smell, color, and visual differentiation. Then there is the behavioral imprinting and habituation which takes place in the early weeks and months of infancy based upon the intimate relationship between the mother and the infant. This helps to ensure that when sexual mating is eventually attempted, it will take place only with those forms that resemble the parent or siblings.[2]

Not surprisingly, the Jews have gone all out to corrupt and cripple the latter tendency in Whites, particularly under the guise of "children's entertainment." In 1994, for example, the Walt Disney Company brought out a re-adaptation of its 1967 film *The Jungle Book*. This was Disney's first children's offering since being taken over by the Jewish clique headed by Michael Eisner, and, predictably, it was a complete distortion, both of the original Kipling story and the 1967 Disney animated version. With a story line remarkably similar to *Last of the Mohicans,* the White heroine rejects her British-officer fiancé for an Indian jungle boy played by a Chinese actor.

Significantly, the White girl's decision is portrayed as being based upon moral considerations of right and wrong, upon her realization that White society and White men in particular are irredeemably bad. Eisner pursued this line in the two subsequent Disney animated children's films, *Pocahontas* and *The Hunchback of Notre Dame,* which are similar both in their pernicious race-mixing propaganda and in their blatant disregard for the original stories. Such systematic consistency in shape and content suggests design rather than coincidence.

In any case, the actual motivation of Michael Eisner in churning out such material is not the most important question. The thing that really matters is the actual effect of his efforts: young children are being influenced, at an age where they are most open to behavioral imprinting, with a message that miscegenation is good and morally correct, and that Whiteness is evil and morally wrong.

Just as young Whites in the past were encouraged by an alien religious dogma to feel sinful because of their natural sexual urges, to feel unclean in having them, and to seek "salvation" by denying them, so today they are indoctrinated with guilt-inducing ideas about being White. And the solution which they are offered to overcome these artificial feelings of guilt and self-hate is increasingly clear: mate with a non-White partner and have mongrel offspring. Racial suicide is thus insidiously presented to them as the only way in which they can overcome their Whiteness and all the consequent pain and shame that goes with it.

THE RELIGION OF THE NEW WORLD ORDER

Actually, miscegenation has rapidly emerged as the official religion of the New World Order and its adherents. Propagated with an increasingly hysterical fervor, it has been developed as the new universal slave-morality which embraces and transcends established religions such as Christianity. In March 1994, for example, evangelist Billy Graham's publication *Christianity Today* urged readers to rejoice over the existence of mixed-race marriages and mixed-race children and to do everything possible to make them fully accepted into society. It even stated that this is one area where the news and entertainment media are morally ahead of the churches.

This propagation of miscegenation as an ideological crusade also has made significant inroads into the education system. When a North Carolina middle school principal recently cautioned a White female student and a Black male student about the dangers of interracial dating, he was immediately suspended from his job and disciplined. He was not allowed to return to work until he had been "reeducated" after confessing and repenting his "sins" in a counseling and sensitivity training program.[3]

The ideological nature of this campaign to promote miscegenation was also reflected in an article in the August 1996 issue of *Maryland Family Magazine,* part of the Times Mirror group. Written by Helen Arminger, described as a candidate for ordained ministry in the United Methodist Church, "How to Raise an Unbiased Child" argues that society is compelled to teach its youth to live harmoniously and productively within a global environment. Quoting approvingly a Maryland education official, Arminger insisted that there exists a moral obligation to provide children with the opportunity to engage in a variety of relationships with people of different races and sexual orientations without any kind of parental or social constraint.

Behind the high-sounding slogans portraying miscegenation as morally imperative and beneficial, the motivation of its proponents is clear: the intention is not to "save" or "redeem" Whites, but to destroy them completely. What such "morality" really derives from is a totally subjective, alien mind-set which seeks the biological extinction of the White race, and which, from its own perspective, sees such an extinction as a good and righteous thing. Some of its proponents are much more honest than others in admitting to this reality. One journal, *Race Traitor*, edited by Noel Ignatiev and subtitled "Treason to Whiteness is Loyalty to Humanity," openly declares its conviction that the only way to solve the social problems of the age is to abolish the White race. Its admitted aim is not "multiculturalism" or "multiracialism," but biological unity and racelessness.[4]

Such thinking is not confined to the political fringes. On September 29, 1996, the *New York Times Magazine* ran an article by Jewish writer Stanley Crouch (author of the book *The All-American Skin Game: Or, the Decoy of Race*). Entitled "Race is Over," Crouch's article confidently predicted that a century from today unprecedented levels of racial mixing—of a wide variety of combinations—will ensure that the very concept of race will be redundant. Americans of the future, it argues, will find themselves surrounded in every direction by people who are part Asian, part Latin, part European, part American Indian. The sweep of body types, combinations of facial features, hair textures, eye colors, and what are now "unexpected skin tones" will, in Crouch's view, be far more common because the current paranoia over mixed marriages should be by then largely a superstition of the past.

Even this declared goal, however, reveals only part of the agenda, because one particular race has an exemption ticket from this universal morality of genetic amalgamation. But the *New York Times Magazine* article symbolizes what the Politically Correct movement is really all about. When the mainstream *Harper's Magazine* runs articles advocating government-sponsored summer camps for young White girls to meet and begin relationships with non-White males, it is not doing "good" for those girls; it is actively encouraging what is most definitely bad for them. And when the Prudential Insurance Company of America sponsors a series of racial unity conferences for children across America and the world, it is not doing what is "right" for those children; it is doing what is totally and utterly wrong for them.

Actually, such "morality" is without any moral foundation whatsoever. It's not based on any natural or biological law, nor does it follow any rational or scientific line of reasoning. This helps to explain why it is having some difficulty in achieving its objectives. Undoubtedly many Whites preach the cause of miscegenation, and many have put it into practice. But, revealingly, the numbers in the latter camp are still much smaller than in the former. Some of the Whites who advocate race-mixing are obviously unhealthy in a genetic sense, and mentally ill as opposed to spiritually sick. The person who wrote to his local newspaper recently stating his frustrated wish to have five per cent Black blood in his ancestry so as to blend in with what he considers the ideal American racial composition may be an example.[5]

In any case, in instances such as these miscegenation could even be considered a tool of natural selection in weeding such people out of the White gene pool.

THE DESIRE TO BE FASHIONABLE

For the majority of Whites who advocate miscegenation, however, their sense of righteousness in espousing it is nothing more than a manifestation of trendiness: of wanting to feel and appear fashionable.

Take, for example, the case of the young Hollywood couple Tom Cruise and Nicole Kidman. Both appear to be healthy and physically attractive specimens of Aryan humanity. Yet they have recently adopted a Black child and actively collaborated with the Jewish media in publicizing it as a fine and noble deed which has helped the cause of human and societal "progress." There is nothing biologically wrong with this couple; they've just gone out of their way to make a fashion statement. And the adopted child is nothing more than a fashion accessory for their symbolic commitment to the idea of miscegenation.

Indeed, it is revealing that for all their fashion consciousness, Cruise and Kidman chose to marry each other rather than non-Whites [they later divorced]; they chose to adopt a non-White child rather than to create one. Even they, therefore, whether conscious of it or not, are evidence that most Whites are not yet putting the idea of miscegenation into practice— regardless of the lip service which they might feel compelled to give it.

A recent study of miscegenation statistics by Jewish academic Douglas J. Besherov, resident scholar at the American Enterprise Institute, seemed to give some credence to this view, although the report highlighted some very disturbing trends. These included a tripling of marriages between Whites and Blacks since 1970, and a sharp increase in marriages between Whites and Asians or Hispanics. The U.S. Census Bureau counted about 150,000 interracial marriages nationwide in 1960. By 1990 that number grew tenfold to 1.5 million. In 1994 it was estimated at more than 3 million.

Equally alarming was the statistic that 35.4 percent of White women married to Black men said they planned to have children, a higher proportion than the 29 percent of White women married to White men who said they wanted children. This is on top of a four-fold increase in mixed-race births since 1970, although not all of these involved a White parent.

OMINOUS TRENDS?

Such trends are obviously ominous and potentially catastrophic by pointing in the long term to the biological extinction of

White America. In the short term, however, from the perspective of those of us trying to prevent such a nightmare from unfolding, they do provide at least some grounds for optimism and opportunity. Despite 30 years of Judeo-Christian brainwashing, over 90 per cent of Whites are declining to transgress what Douglas J. Besherov admits is American society's "last taboo."

Similarly, despite the efforts of Senator Howard Metzenbaum (D-OH, now retired), who in 1994 introduced the Multiethnic Placement Act in the Senate in an effort to bring about an increase in transracial adoptions, most Whites appear still to prefer to adopt White babies, and most non-Whites still prefer to adopt non-White babies. Such attitudes, moreover, appear to be hardening in spite of the Clinton administration's attempts to legislate against them. The Cruise-Kidman adoption, for instance, was condemned by the National Association of Black Social Workers on the grounds that transracial adoptions amounted to racial and cultural genocide.

Undoubtedly an important factor in this situation has been the growth in tensions that has accompanied the transition to a multiracial society. As racial and ethnic identification has become more relevant in people's lives, the resulting racial polarization and intensified group solidarity have mitigated somewhat against the idea of interracial mating. It seems clear, for example, that the O.J. Simpson trial served the useful purpose of intensifying both White and Black racial consciousness and of discrediting the idea of miscegenation.

One hopeful sign of this was the fact that Hulond Humphries, a White high school principal in Wedowee, Alabama, who was ousted from his position in 1994 for threatening to cancel the spring prom if interracial couples turned up, recently won an election runoff for superintendent of schools.

As with the race question in general, many Whites—for the moment at least—seem to be carrying around with them two conflicting value systems in relation to race-mixing: the one they publicly purport to hold and the one they actually live their private lives by. While the former is artificially created and only maintained by continuous external conditioning, the latter arises from instinct, which is genetically ingrained.

Thus, although race-mixing propaganda may have been purposefully designed to appeal to the subconscious and to avoid encountering rational faculties, it has inevitably come up against subconscious genetic realities which are not easily influenced by alien attempts at behavioral modification. Consequently, while it has been relatively easy to bring about widescale spiritual sickness and confusion, it has been much more difficult to implement widescale biological amalgamation.

Such a situation, however, will not last forever. History is full of examples of artificial and destructive moralities triumphing over the natural order. Despite its setbacks, the cult of miscegenation has spread substantially over the last thirty years and will continue to do so. Current trends continue to point to the most fundamental and inescapable reality which confronts us today: the White race stands on the precipice of biological extinction.

And one thing is certain: as the strains and tensions of this multiracial society increase in the coming years, so the campaign to destroy us through racial mixing will intensify. For this reason alone, regardless of increased racial polarization, the false morality of miscegenation will not disappear naturally. The circumstances of racial chaos will help us, but only organized and radical action on our part will achieve the vital necessity of a complete and decisive separation of the races and the final destruction of the morality of death.

NOTES

1. *Newsweek*, June 10, 1991.
2. Roger Pearson, 'Ecology, Adaptation, and Speciation,' in *Ecology and Evolution*, Washington, DC (1996).
3. Raleigh *News and Record*, February 10, 1996.
4. *Race Traitor*, No. 2, Winter 1993.
5. Letter from Ivan Wittman to Pittsburgh *Post-Gazette*, May 4, 1996.

The New White Nationalists: Jared Taylor and the *American Renaissance* Crowd

LEONARD ZESKIND

Some contemporary white separatists distinguish themselves from neo-Nazis, Klansmen, Christian Identity adherents, and other militants who align themselves with the political far right, writes Leonard Zeskind in the following selection. Such is the case with a group of highly educated journalists, politicians, clergymen, and professors who are affiliated with Jared Taylor and his *American Renaissance* newsletter. Taylor and colleagues such as Sam Francis often maintain that different races have different intellectual abilities, that blacks are inherently prone to crime, and that Euro-American civilization is threatened by multiculturalism and immigration, Zeskind explains. Eschewing violence, the *"American Renaissance* crowd" seeks to influence public debate and conservative politics. Zeskind is president of the Institute for Research and Education on Human Rights.

A resurgent white racial consciousness is afoot, eschewing the militia look. Over Memorial Day weekend [in 1996], Samuel Jared Taylor's *American Renaissance* newsletter will convene 150 university professors, journalists and clergymen in Louisville, Kentucky's Seelbach Hotel for gentlemanly discussion—coats and ties required. They will catalogue a growing list of indecencies, including theft of the national shrines by

Excerpted from "White-Shoed Supremacy: A Resurgent Racial Consciousness Is Afoot, Eschewing the Militia Look," by Leonard Zeskind, *Nation*, June 10, 1996. Copyright © 1996 by Nation Magazine. Reprinted with permission.

bands of multicultural brigands and an imminent demographic tsunami that will swamp European-Americans altogether. They will lament the demographic link between the black race, crime and I.Q. as a sobering but scientific fact.

At the end, a solution will present itself: resurgent white racial consciousness as a precursor to old-fashioned white supremacy. Nothing hateful, mind you, just the stuff that once made America great. They call it "white separatism" now.

THE VANGUARD OF THE FAR RIGHT

This is not just another gathering of crackpots. Many of the *American Renaissance* crowd come from respectable institutions. And thanks to the presidential campaign of Pat Buchanan, whom many of them have supported and informally advised, the wind is at their backs. Their rise is emblematic of a re-alignment on the right: a break in the ranks of religious and cultural conservatives and the emergence of a new white nationalism as a credible autonomous movement. Although weakened by the infantilism of its militia wing, the new white nationalists will increasingly act as the vanguard of the far right.

More a brain trust for a neo-Confederate national revival than an Aryan Nations militia outpost, the Memorial Day conference will be a reprise of a 1994 Atlanta meeting. At that time Taylor, a handsome middle-aged Japan expert and Anglophile Yalie, introduced a small contingent of Northern Jews and Catholics to his Southern brethren. Rabbi Meyer Schiller from Yeshiva University High School in Queens, Fr. Ronald Tacelli S.J. from Boston University and CUNY prof. Michael Levin spoke to a crowd that included Ed Fields, publisher of *The Truth At Last,* a baldly anti-Semitic tabloid popular at cross-burnings. For some reason, David Duke was turned away.

Sam Dickson, an Atlanta lawyer whose hobby is casting doubt on the Holocaust at his own Historical Review Press, was my favorite of the weekend. He skewered the left-wing portrait of right-wingers as paranoid and status-anxious. Tactfully, Dickson left the business about Hitler and genocide at home. A supporter of David Duke's campaigns for state representative and Louisiana governor, he gave $250 to Pat Buchanan's presidential bid in 1995.

Dickson isn't the only Old South type to support Buchanan's presidential aspirations. Among them is Boyd Cathey, former editor of *Southern Partisan,* a glossy quarterly magazine devoted to sectional irredentism and re-doing the War Between the States. Cathey was the North Carolina state chairman for Buchanan in 1992. Three years earlier, he joined the twenty-five-member advisory board of the Institute for Historical Review in California, which maintains that the Nazis didn't do it. He claims to have left the advisory board in 1992, although he is still listed on institute publications. He and Buchanan are now two of *Southern Partisan's* three "senior advisors."

A FOOT IN THE CONSERVATIVE DOOR

When Taylor first started *American Renaissance* in 1990, he stuck to the usual right-wing litany of complaints about black people and affirmative action, without much hint of the genetic determinism that distinguishes white supremacists from ordinary racists. His 1992 book was similarly cast; in a review in *The Wall Street Journal,* Clint Bolick of the Institute for Justice called it "easily the most comprehensive indictment of . . . race-conscious civil rights policies."

Then came *The Bell Curve,* which altered the debate on the right about race. [*The Bell Curve* by Charles Murray and Richard Herrnstein is a 1994 book that argues that different races have different intellectual abilities.] Now it's O.K. to say what could only be intimated in the past. As *American Renaissance* concluded in December 1994, "The rules of dialogue in America may finally have changed . . . by injecting questions of race and intelligence into the mainstream, [*The Bell Curve*] has done the country an enormous service." Everyone get out your yardsticks; science is at hand. "Larger heads (containing larger brains) are positively correlated with intelligence," Taylor wrote in a book review in that same issue. "As groups, whites and Asians have larger brains than blacks."

At the same time, Taylor has stripped anti-Semitism, if not

anti–Semites, from the mix. By keeping the conversation in Atlanta well-mannered and heavily referenced, he stuck a decidedly white supremacist foot in the door of a mainstream conservative movement that still bars the bedsheet and brownshirt crowd.

One of the first to sense the wind shift was Sam Francis, a longtime friend and informal adviser to Pat Buchanan. While Francis wasn't certain that race was a "sufficient" cause of white accomplishment, it certainly was a "necessary" one. "The civilization that we as whites created in Europe and America could not have developed apart from the genetic endowments of the creating people," he told the Renaissancers in 1994. At that time, Taylor had just raised the white nationalist sail, which is now filling with the wind from Buchanan's America First campaign.

At the Populist Party's national convention in Allentown, Pennsylvania in September 1995, Kirk Lyons gave a long, boring presentation to 150 of the faithful on Janet Reno's Waco "holocaust," complete with pointer and diagrams projected on the wall. The North Carolina attorney and Aryan Nations parade marshal was hoping to generate support for his lawsuits against the Feds. Michigan militiameister Mark Koernke's speech was even more of a sleeper, with a predictable set of slogans about the United Nations and the New World Order.

Not to be confused with the party of William Jennings Bryan, the contemporary Populist Party started in 1984 as an aggregation of "white citizen" types, Christian patriots and lapsed Klansmen. Its best-known presidential candidate was David Duke in 1988, shortly before he became a Republican. In 1992 the party sponsored Bo Gritz's Rambo-style campaign for President, but managed to get ballot status in only eighteen states. At the September 1995 convention, completely out of gas, it endorsed Buchanan and then disbanded.

American Renaissancer Taylor did his stump speech about black people and crime, focusing everybody's anxiety on the threat from one step below them on the social ladder. Sam

Francis, on the other hand, turned everybody's attention to the danger a step or two up. Political, economic and cultural elites were "actively anti-American," he said. Corporate C.E.O.s were driving wages down to the level of Third World countries and "doing everything they can to actually abolish the culture and civilization and the very population that created the nation and civilization" through increased nonwhite immigration.

MIDDLE AMERICAN RADICALS

Taylor and Francis had their fingers on the hot button for Buchanan's 1992 and 1996 primary bids. His core constituency feels sandwiched between economic and political elites on one side and poor blacks, Latinos and Asians on the other. Fear of this Scylla and Charybdis is a defining feature of Middle American Radicals, or MARs. MARs were discovered by Michigan sociologist Donald Warren in his 1976 study of George Wallace's presidential campaigns, The Radical Center. Warren identified them as middle-class political radicals who believe that "the rich give in to the demands of the poor, and the middle income people have to pay the bill." In 1968 and 1972 MARsians supported Wallace, in the eighties they were Reagan Democrats and in the nineties they voted for Ross Perot and Pat Buchanan.

Although Warren said they are most heavily concentrated in the South, Middle American Radicals are found everywhere. They can be spotted at gun shows and militia meets, at Tenth Amendment rallies and flying the Confederate battle flag. MARsians carried Proposition 187 across the finish line in California. [In 1994, California voters passed Proposition 187, a measure that would deny illegal immigrants the use of non-emergency public health services and public education. The measure was eventually declared unconstitutional.] Even "the religious right is itself a Middle American movement," if you believe Sam Francis.

Francis is the philosopher-general of Middle American Radicalism. A sharp-witted history Ph.D. from the University of North Carolina, he was recruited to be Senator John East's legislative assistant in the eighties. Francis then spent nine years as an editorial writer at *The Washington Times*. There he struck up his friendship with fellow columnist Pat Buchanan. When Buchanan surrendered his column to run for President in 1991, Francis took it over. Last year, after his remarks at the 1994 Atlanta meeting were criticized by Dinesh D'Souza, who attended the conference, the *Times* demoted Francis. Later, when he ridiculed Southern Baptists for deciding that slavery was a sin, Francis was forced to resign. He kept his syndicated column, however, as well as a monthly soapbox at *Chronicles,* the paleo-conservative magazine of choice.

"What has happened in the Buchanan revolution," Francis wrote in 1992, "is the emergency of a new political identity . . . of a particular cultural and political force—Middle America—as the defining core."

Francis hopes that the Middle American Radicals will oppose what he argues is a deracinated new managerial class that has seized the federal government's reins and abandoned Anglo-Saxonism for an antinationalist New World Order. As he writes in his 1993 book, *Beautiful Losers,* changes in the economy had marginalized the old industrial barons and their allies on Main Street who protected the Old Republic before World War II. Francis believes that Middle Americanism is the only line of defense against the elites' surrender of national sovereignty to the multicultural invasion.

Francis's analysis of U.S. racial nationalism replaces Marx's internationalist proletariat with a nationalist white middle class as the agency of change. His friend Pat Buchanan would lead a revolutionary transitional government. An unknown Lenin is presumably still waiting in the wings.

"The reason Buchanan has not been submerged is that the torch he carries illuminates new social forces," Francis boasted in the March 1996 issue of *Chronicles.* "The Buchanan campaign for the first time in recent history offers them an organized mode of expression that will allow them to develop and mature their consciousness and power."

XENOPHOBIA

Is Francis right? Does Buchanan's campaign represent a singular, but still inchoate, Middle Americanism? For Buchanan, foreign trade and immigration, like abortion and even jobs, are battlegrounds in one single cultural war fought by Middle American Radicals. Pat knows that "the great disputed province of American politics is this angry alienated middle class." And he realizes that what appears to be an economic issue to elites is at heart a cultural-national issue to the MARs. That is why his response to economic distress is not job creation or raising wages or promoting unions but xenophobia.

"Today, illegal immigration is helping fuel the cultural breakdown of our nation," Buchanan wrote in October 1994. "That cultural breakdown, which you and I have recognized and sworn to fight, is the single most important factor which has impelled me to run for President." Sam Francis understands his old friend. "For Buchanan . . . the nation is fundamentally a social and cultural unit, not the creation of the state and its policies."

But for Francis, as we have already seen, race should be added to the list of ingredients for a nation. He hasn't yet succeeded in pushing Pat over that line. That's what the next four years [1996–2000] will be about for Buchananites: whether the new white nationalists can win terrain currently held by cultural conservatives. Much will depend on the political maturity of white supremacist cadres who have become Buchananites and joined the Republican Party like latter-day Trotskyists practicing a new form of entryism.

CHAPTER 5

PERSONAL NARRATIVES AND PERSPECTIVES ON WHITE SEPARATISM

AMERICAN
SOCIAL
MOVEMENTS

The Beginning of My Transformation

DAVID DUKE

A former leader of both the Louisiana Knights of the Ku Klux Klan and the National Association for the Advancement of White People, David Duke was elected to the Louisiana House of Representatives in 1989 and made an unsuccessful bid for U.S. Senator in 1990. In the following selection, excerpted from his autobiography *My Awakening*, Duke describes how the mainstream pro-integration media influenced his views when he was a youth. Duke maintains that he believed in racial equality until he was challenged by a homework assignment that required him to find arguments against racial integration. When he read Carleton Putnam's book *Race and Reason*, he discovered that many of America's Founding Fathers did not believe in the equality of the races, and he was exposed to theories about genetic differences between the blacks and whites. Putnam's ideas led Duke to question his former belief in racial egalitarianism.

"Never run from the truth," Pinky told me. She encouraged me to admit to my folks that I had accidentally broken an old porcelain figurine they treasured. "What would Jesus say about that?" she added. I ultimately admitted my transgression to my folks and faced punishment, but I had to admit that it was better to take my medicine than to live a lie.

Our Black housekeeper, Pinky, always gave me advice such as "never run from the truth." After our return from Holland, she was the closest woman to me other than Mother and my sister, Dotti. My folks hired her to take care of the house and to watch over Dotti and me, but none of us really looked upon her as an employee. When she stayed late, we always insisted that she eat supper with us, and my father expected her to join us at the table.

Often Mother, with me tagging along, drove her home into one of the blackest parts of New Orleans, the lower Claiborne Avenue area. This was in the late '50s, when one could travel such streets safely, before the advent of the "love and brotherhood" brought by the civil-rights movement.

Pinky had the same authority over me that Mother and Father had. If I didn't obey her, my folks would punish me just as if I had disobeyed them. Pinky did housework and prepared snacks for me. We had conversations about a thousand and one subjects. She always attempted to derive every opinion from a solid Christian point of view. Scolding me for improper behavior, she would always intone, "What would Jesus say about that?" The words were really in the form of a declaration rather than a question, for the answer was always obvious: "Jesus would not approve." To Pinky there were no shades of gray to any ethical question, only clear right or wrong. Pinky influenced me to be opinionated—to think an issue over and then take a definite position rather than just sit on the fence. This is a trait that has stayed with me. Concerning racial issues, Pinky had a traditional southern Black attitude. She insisted on using the toilet in the utility room rather than the main bathroom, and if we picked up some takeout food at a restaurant, she always used the "colored" service area. She was opposed to socializing with White folks other than in her work.

One day I asked Pinky why she had no problem with segregation. She answered simply and eloquently, "Cause I want to be with my *own* kind." Although she was not of my "*own kind*," when she died, and I looked into her open coffin at her kind face, I saw only someone for whom I cared and who cared for me. She was someone who had made me laugh, who punished me when I went wrong, and who had encouraged me when she saw me doing something responsible or creative. . . .

THE CIVIL-RIGHTS MOVEMENT

As I grew older the civil-rights movement was maturing as well, and by the time I was 11, the South was in turmoil. A social structure that had existed for hundreds of years was being completely overturned at an astonishing speed. At first I did very little thinking on the race question. I was far more concerned with my love of the outdoors, science, and my escapist world of reading (mostly of scientific books and only a little political material).

Instinctively, because of my love for the Confederacy, I initially identified with the traditionally conservative position of the South in opposition to racial integration. I saw the civil-rights movement simply as a destruction of our Southern way of life, but I hadn't thought very deeply about the issue. As civil-rights pushed to the forefront of the news in the early '60s, I began to read a great deal about the issue in newspapers and magazines, and as I did I grew more sympathetic toward the Negro cause.

Practically everything written about the subject in books, newspaper and magazine articles, as well as everything on television—led me to believe that the civil-rights movement was based on lofty principles of justice and human rights. The media proclaimed that these policies would lead America to racial harmony and material progress.

I read articles proclaiming that there is no significant genetic difference between Whites and Blacks other than skin color. Racial differences in poverty, illegitimacy, crime rates, drug addiction, educational failure, were said to be caused purely by environmental differences among the races. The media blamed Black failure and dysfunction on segregation and White racism. Ultimately, the poor circumstances of Black people were blamed squarely on White evil. . . .

Some stories were about the suppression of Blacks in slavery and about discrimination and brutality against Blacks since emancipation. The heart-rending accounts would provoke sympathy and outrage in any person sensitive to human suffering. At the same time I came across articles about the "great

Black civilizations of Africa" and the "great Blacks in American history.". . . .

THE IMPACT OF THE MEDIA

Even my patriotic values were enlisted in the cause of racial integration. I read articles in major magazines that maintained that racial equality is proclaimed in the Constitution of the United States. And frequently quoted were the well-known words of the Declaration of Independence, "We hold these truths to be self-evident, that all men are created equal. . . ."

In addition to Thomas Jefferson's words in the Declaration of Independence, the following line was used repeatedly in articles: "Nothing is more certainly written in the book of fate than that these people (the Negroes) are to be free." One summer I traveled with Father to Washington, D.C., and saw those very words inscribed in magnificent foot–tall letters on the inspiring Jefferson Memorial on the Potomac. In the Gettysburg Address, which was quoted almost as often as the Declaration of Independence, Lincoln seemingly paid homage to the concept of racial equality: "Four score and seven years ago our fathers brought forth on this continent a new nation, conceived in liberty and dedicated to the proposition that all men are *created equal.*"

For a fiercely patriotic young man who idolized men like Davy Crockett, Teddy Roosevelt, Thomas Jefferson and Abraham Lincoln, these quotations were very persuasive. My belief that America's greatest heroes had endorsed racial equality helped influence my own attitudes.

Integration of public schools was a major issue at this time, and the media portrayed it as a good thing for America. Judging by what I saw on television, integration simply meant one or two little Black girls seeking to attend a formerly all White school. On the opposite hand Whites were shown unchivalrously screaming racist invectives—and attacking the quiet and well-dressed Negro children being escorted into school.

Over the years I saw on TV and read hundreds of dramatic portrayals of Blacks being hurt, oppressed, enslaved, discriminated against, falsely accused, whipped, lynched, spat upon, raped and ridiculed. Because I was idealistic and aspired to be fair and generous and chivalrous—and because I was under the influence of the media—I came to believe that racial integration would elevate the Black people to their true ability and thereby guarantee justice for them and progress for all.

There is no exaggerating the impact of television during the '50s and '60s on the issue of integration. The newness of live television coming into the home sanctified the media newscaster and made him seem bigger than life. In awe of the technology, many people uncritically accepted what they were fed through their televisions. I was no exception....

AN INTERESTING HOMEWORK ASSIGNMENT
In an eighth-grade civics class at Ganus Junior High School, the teacher gave her students an interesting assignment. We were to choose a topic dealing with current events and take a polemical position on it, then research that topic and defend it rationally in class. I chose as my topic "The Case for Racial Integration of Education." After each of us had chosen and taken a position, she told us that we had probably taken a topic we probably agreed with. So our assignment now became to research and take the opposite point of view from what we had originally chosen. The assignment set my mind in turmoil. I went to the school library that afternoon to research "The Case *Against* Racial Integration of Education." In the card file I found listed many books on the subjects of racial equality and integration of education. I had, evidently, chosen a topic that would be easily researched. But as I examined the books, I found that one after another argued in favor of integration. Even in this small church-school library, there were at least a dozen books promoting the civil-rights movement and its heroes, but *no* books on the other side. Why? It was obvious that there was a lot of popular opposition to integration. I had seen the newsreels of its White opponents, and segregationists were being elected all over the South. Whites rioted in New Orleans to prevent integration of the schools and almost every

major politician of the time opposed it in principle. Yet, amazingly, I couldn't find a book against it.

The next day I went to the Doubleday bookstore on Canal Street hoping to search out some books opposed to forced integration of public education. I found dozens of books promoting integration, and some even touting Black supremacy. But again, I found nothing opposed to integration. Even the books that supposedly offered a balanced analysis of the issue were decidedly one-sided in their presentation. Finally, to make some progress on my assignment, I resorted to gleaning the *anti*-integration arguments from *pro*-integration books.

Those arguments were uneven. The liberal civil-rights books made the arguments of segregationists seem stupid and banal. I read that Whites are opposed to integration because of sexual insecurity; that Whites want to oppress Blacks so they can keep them economically subjugated and exploited (The Marxist interpretation); that segregationists hate Blacks simply because of their color. A few of the books suggested that some segregationists thought that Blacks were less intelligent and more violent than Whites—a distinction that they argued would lead to a marked decline in American education. The liberals curtly dismissed such arguments by saying that "no scientific evidence supports the contention that Whites are smarter than Blacks," and they repeated in a litany, "The only difference is the color of skin." I was in a quandary. I had to defend a position that had no supporting evidence and one that I morally opposed. When I opened the morning paper a few days before my school assignment was due, I saw something that gave me a glimmer of hope. The *Times-Picayune* reported a meeting held at the Municipal Auditorium by the New Orleans chapter of the White Citizens Council. It quoted Judge Leander Perez of Plaquemines Parish as saying that racial integration would ultimately destroy the quality of the New Orleans public school system.

There was little of substance in the news article, but learning about the existence of the Citizens Council heightened my hopes of finding information from the segregationist viewpoint. After school I rode the old Canal Street streetcar downtown to the Citizens Council offices on Carondolet Street, expecting only to find a few obscure and discredited sources for the segregationist position.

A middle-aged woman, Mrs. Singleton, with bleached-out freckles and bifocals greeted me with a deep Southern accent more characteristic of neighboring Mississippi than of New Orleans. She was busy with a mailing, so I hurriedly asked if she had any books that opposed the integration of education. With a slightly exasperated manner, she pointed to bookshelves that were ten feet tall and stretched across an entire wall 15 feet across. "Take a look," she snapped.

What I saw amazed me. They had hundreds of volumes that supported the idea that racial differences go far beyond skin color; that heredity rather than environment are the key shapers of intelligence and personality; and that there is a historical record of racial integration and intermarriage in many nations that indicates racial mixing retards progress and leads to lowering standards.

I looked over books by prominent geneticists, psychologists, anthropologists, historians, sociologists and educators. They took the point of view that no matter how we might wish it otherwise, *race does matter*. A book by Audrey Shuey, *The Testing of Negro Intelligence,* assembled 384 separate scientific studies on intelligence and race, all of them showing a marked difference between the races. Another book that caught my eye was *Race, Riots and Revolution* by Teddy Roosevelt, a president whom I idolized for his conservationism and patriotism.

All of this came as a shock to me. I found an opposing viewpoint on racial integration that is literate, reasoned and intelligent—even supported by famous Americans—not simply the ranting of backwoods White supremacists. It is a viewpoint on race the popular media in America would not even acknowledge. I didn't have much money—it was 1963 and I was 13 years old—so I asked the lady at the desk which book she would recommend. She picked up a paperback copy of *Race and Reason: A Yankee View* by Carleton Putnam and put it in a bag for me with a handwritten receipt.

The voice of Pinky crept into my mind as I walked to the Canal Street streetcar, and I wondered if I betrayed her memory by even reading such material. Was I doing her some wrong even to consider the idea that the races differ?

But then Pinky's admonishment never to run from the truth came back to me as if she had been right there speaking those words again from her own mouth. If I should not run from the truth, then I sure should not be afraid to confront a falsehood either. I imagined *Race and Reason* would be an easily refutable, shallow exposition of race prejudice. All the same, I had an uneasy feeling about it. I had no inkling, when I walked out of the drab little office on Carondolet Street, that I was about to read a book that would change my life.

READING *RACE AND REASON*

The book riveted me. I read it on the streetcar, and then on the connecting bus all the way home, almost missing my stop. When I walked home from the bus stop, I would pause and read a couple of paragraphs and then close the book and walk while I thought about the concept. That evening, after wolfing down my supper, I bounded upstairs to my bedroom where I retrieved my book from its paper bag and read until I finished it.

The book did not convert me, but it made me think critically for the first time about the race issue, and it made me question the egalitarian arguments that I had uncritically accepted. I was not ready to give up my egalitarian beliefs, but *Race and Reason* made me realize another legitimate and scientific point of view existed.

I asked myself, *What if the things he writes are true? What if the distinctions, quality and composition of races are the primary factors in the vitality of civilizations?*

Putnam prophesied that massive racial integration of American public schools would lead to increasing Black racism, resentment and frustration, reduced educational standards, increased violence in the schools, and a resulting implosion of the great cities of America. I worried that such a fate could befall our country. I wanted to find out the truth, no matter where it might lead.

One allegation by Putnam especially interested me. He said that most of America's Founding Fathers were convinced believers in racial differences and that even President Lincoln, the Great Emancipator, stated repeatedly that he believed that there were wide differences in the races that make necessary their separation. If Putnam's allegations were correct, then I would have to acknowledge that the media had deceived me on an important matter. My generation had been taught that racial equality was enshrined in the principles of our Founding Fathers and supposedly represented even by the *Declaration of Independence:* "We hold these truths to be self-evident, that all men are created equal, that they are endowed by their Creator with certain unalienable rights. . . ."

Most Americans can instantly identify these words. But do these words mean that Jefferson and the other patriots who put their names on that document believed that all men were truly created biologically equal; that the White and Black races had equal endowments from the Creator?

How could that be true, asked Putnam, when the same document refers to Indians as "merciless savages" who massacred innocents without regard to age or gender?

> He has excited domestic insurrections amongst us, and has endeavoured to bring on the inhabitants of our frontiers, the merciless Indian Savages, whose known rule of warfare, is an undistinguished destruction of all ages, sexes and conditions.

Anyone who used such language today from the podium of the Republican or Democratic National Convention would be universally scorned.

How could they really believe in racial equality, when many of the signers themselves, including the author, Thomas Jefferson, owned Black slaves that were considered chattel property? What of their slaves' unalienable rights? Were our Founding Fathers blatant hypocrites, or did the declaration simply say that our rights as British subjects in the thirteen Colonies were the same as those of our British brothers back in England?

JEFFERSON'S WORDS

After I read and re-read the rest of Jefferson's utterances on the Negro question, it seemed certain to me that he was not referring to racial equality when he penned the Declaration of Independence. Other than the "created equal" line in the *Declaration of Independence,* the most common quote by any American Founding Father used to bolster the civil-rights movement was Jefferson's classic line that reads: "Nothing is more certainly written in the book of fate, than that these people [the Negroes] are to be free."

This declamation has been used in thousands of books, articles, plays, documentaries and movies—more than any other famous enunciation on the race issue. On the beautiful Jefferson Memorial in Washington, it is found chiseled as sacred writ on the huge interior panels of granite. The next sentence on the wall begins with the word education. In media articles the quotation ends with the words "are to be free." Neither the articles nor the memorial's architect give the public the honesty of an ellipsis, for the quotation is clearly an intentional deception that completely alters his original meaning.

The quotation itself is only a fragment of one of Jefferson's sentences written in his autobiography:

> Nothing is more certainly written in the book of fate than that these people [Negroes] are to be free. Nor is it less certain that the two races, equally free, cannot live in the same government. Nature, habit, opinion has drawn indelible lines of distinction between them.

When I first read the complete text of the Jefferson statement, it stunned me. Not only did Jefferson not believe in racial equality, he stated clearly that Nature had made the Black and White races so indelibly different that they couldn't live in the same government, and that unless the Black race was returned to Africa, he "shuddered" for America's future. The egalitarian sources that wrote loftily of his belief in equality had brazenly deceived me.

Perhaps Jefferson was wrong in his opinion, I thought, but why have his words been twisted completely opposite to his original intent? I remembered my visit to the rotunda of the Jefferson Memorial, when I had stared up in reverence at those words across from the magnificent statue of Jefferson himself. Now, I knew those words etched in granite were a lie.

The rest of those powerful words had simply gone down what the writer George Orwell called the "memory hole" in his classic book *1984*. If the establishment would blatantly suppress and distort a historical fact as important as this, I wondered if there were other important deceptions about race. Putnam exposed many more.

LINCOLN'S SENTIMENTS

Martin Luther King's 1964 Civil Rights March on Washington held its rally at the Lincoln Memorial. I knew that Lincoln was opposed to the institution of slavery, as was Jefferson, but what would Lincoln's opinion be on the march for racial integration and racial equality that assembled on the steps of his imposing memorial? Here are some of Lincoln's surprising sentiments on the issue: "Negro equality. Fudge! How long in the Government of a God great enough to make and maintain this Universe, shall there continue knaves to vend and fools to gulp, so low a piece of demagoguism as this?". . .

In the famous Lincoln-Douglas Debates in Charleston, Illinois, Lincoln said:

> I am not, nor ever have been in favor of bringing about in any way the social and political equality of the white and black races. I am not nor ever have been in favor of making voters or jurors of Negroes, nor qualifying them to hold office, nor to intermarry with White people; and I will say in addition to this that there is a physical difference between the white and black races which I believe will ever forbid the two races living together on terms of social and political equality.

In the shadow of the monument to the man who spoke the above words, assembled the 1964 Civil Rights march. The heavens must have laughed in irony. . . .

The "patriotic-American" argument for racial integration, which I had once accepted unquestionably, had collapsed, for if opposing racial integration made one un-American or un-patriotic, then unpatriotic is the man who wrote our Declaration of Independence, the president who ultimately freed the slaves and even the man who composed our national anthem. Our Founding Fathers were not only segregationists in the classic sense, they were White separatists who accurately predicted that the continued presence of Africans in America would lead to intractable social conflict. They believed the only equitable solution could be the repatriation of all Blacks from the United States, and they formed a society to accomplish that purpose. They even acquired land in Africa to become that new nation. In the end they were stymied in their quest, first by the economic power of slaveholders, who sought to preserve their fortunes, and later, at the close of the War for Southern Independence, by radical political forces who used the newly freed slaves as political fodder to maintain their control of the Congress. . . .

As I continued to read and find many more lies and falsehoods about race, my own hostility grew, along with my determination to discover the truth about race, wherever it might lead.

The Cantor and the Klansman

In the following selection, *Time* magazine correspondent Daniel S. Levy interviews Larry Trapp, a former Grand Dragon of the Nebraska Ku Klux Klan, and Michael Weisser, a Jewish cantor living in Lincoln, Nebraska. When Trapp was still active in the Klan, he attempted to intimidate Weisser with hate mail and threatening phone calls. Weisser responded by leaving messages on Trapp's answering machine, assertively challenging Trapp to reconsider the implications of his hateful actions. Eventually the two began a dialogue which grew into a friendship that enabled Trapp to leave the white supremacist movement. Here Trapp and Weisser discuss their unusual relationship and the nature of racist organizations.

Q. Mr. Trapp, when you realized that Michael Weisser lived in your town of Lincoln, Nebraska, you started trying to intimidate him. What were you hoping to achieve?

Larry Trapp: The initial thing is fear, with the intention of getting him out of the community. White supremacists think everything is theirs—the community, the state, everything. As the state leader, the Grand Dragon, I did more than my share of work because I wanted to build up the state of Nebraska into a state as hateful as North Carolina and Florida. I spent a lot of money and went out of my way to instill fear.

Q. When Larry Trapp started harassing and threatening you, what did you do?

Michael Weisser: I called the police, and I had the telephone company put a tap on my telephone. Two days later I got a package of hate mail, anti–Jewish and anti–black material. We knew it was from Larry Trapp, but we couldn't prove it. We were pretty frightened. It went on that way for a while, and then I talked with my wife Julie, and I said I had to confront this. The only thing I hoped to accomplish was to let him know that I wasn't afraid of him. I was pretty angry, but I never expressed any anger on the telephone to him.

Q. Had you actually spoken to him?

Weisser: At first it was just messages. The very first time I reached his answering machine, I had to listen to a 10-minute taped diatribe about how evil the Jews and the blacks were. There was a beep at the end to leave a message, and I said, "Larry, you'd better think about all this hatred you're doing, that you are involved in, because you're going to have to deal with God one day, and it's not going to be easy." Larry is disabled, and another time I called, I said, "Larry, the very first laws that the Nazis passed were against people like yourself, who have physical disabilities, and you would have been among those to die under the Nazis. Why do you love the Nazis so much?"

Trapp: I knew that too.

Weisser: I just kept leaving messages, until finally one day, Larry Trapp, in a fit of anger, picked up the phone. "What do you want?" he said. "You're harassing me! My phone's got a tap on it." I was real quiet and calm. I said I knew he had a hard time getting around and thought he might need a ride to the grocery store. He just got completely quiet, and all the anger went out of his voice, and he said, "I've got that taken care of, but thanks for asking."

Q. Mr. Trapp, what was it that first made you hate?

Trapp: When I was 13 or 14 years old in reform school in Kearney, Neb., I was raped by four or five black boys. From then on I just hated blacks. Every time I was around them, I felt like killing them. Anybody who wasn't like me was my enemy.

Q. Cantor Weisser, over the next few months, the man who considered you his enemy had his doubts about his past and grudgingly accepted your existence. What happened the night you finally met?

Weisser: The phone rang, and Larry said, "I want to get out

of this, and I don't know how." I asked if he had had dinner and said I would bring something over and we'd have a bite to eat and talk about it. I told Julie what had happened, and she said, "I'll bet Larry Trapp is just as apprehensive about us as we are about him. I think we ought to bring him a peace offering." She found a silver ring, and we went over there. As we walked in I touched his hand and he burst into tears. He didn't know we were bringing the ring, and he had two silver swastika rings on, one on each hand. He took the two rings off and said, "I want you to take these rings; they just symbolize hatred and evil, and I want them out of my life." Julie gave him the other ring and put it on his finger.

Q. Mr. Trapp, have you now completely renounced the Klan and the Nazi Party?

Trapp: I denounce everything they stand for. But it's not the people in the organizations that I hate. I hate what they stand for and what they do. If I were to say I hate all Klansmen because they're Klansmen and all Nazis because they're Nazis, I would still be a racist. I was one of the most hardcase white activists in the U. S. If I can have that change of mind or change of heart, anybody can.

Q. There is another former Klansman, David Duke, who claims to have renounced the Klan. How is he different?

Trapp: Racism used to take a more blatant form: the hangings, the beating of blacks half to death on the streets. Listen to David Duke's policies. What he is doing—and I've talked to him personally—what he's doing is using a more subdued racism. If you check his policies closely, you'll find that they're the same policies that they have always been. There is no change.

Q. Should white supremacists be taken seriously?

Trapp: The end goal of the white movement is the complete annihilation of all nonwhites. There is talk of setting up purely white colonies here in the U.S. That way they'll have their economy established when the rest of the U.S. is taken over by the whites. What they are talking about is basically tyranny.

There are books that have been written that are more or less a philosophy of the white movement. They talk about pregnant white women hanging from trees and lampposts with signs on them saying I WAS A RACE TRAITOR, with their belly cut open, their baby cut out. This is what they plan on. They're a bunch of savages.

Q. I understand that you have been threatened since you left the Klan.

Trapp: I really rattled that applecart and caused a lot of damage within the movement by retiring. I'm sure there's a contract out on me. Usually what happens is, the word gets passed around among the skinheads. They're the ones to worry about, because they're the ones who do all the dirty deeds. The skinheads around town know me, and I am not afraid of them.

Q. If a Klansman got in touch with you and said he wanted to leave the organization, would you help him?

Trapp: I'd check him out real good. The Klan pulls a lot of scams on a lot of people, even their own. For years they've been backstabbing themselves. Not one Klansman or one Nazi can really say he actually trusts the other. It's constant conflict. This is one of the reasons they're in a decline.

Q. Do you think the Klan or the Nazi Party will live on?

Trapp: They're going into what they call the Fifth Era. Things are getting kind of bad for them, so they're going to act, and I think it is going to be very soon. I think what they're going to do is get into smaller terrorist groups, and there's going to be a lot of terrorist acts. This is what I fear more than anything.

Q. Cantor Weisser, Larry Trapp once represented a white-cloaked devil to you. How does it feel to realize that he's basically a good man?

Weisser: I think Larry Trapp has always been a good man, yet he's had a life that's been messed up. Until I spoke to Larry Trapp, I'd only had a couple of other experiences with people who are involved in the organizations that Larry was involved with. I never wanted to talk to them; I was afraid of them. The experience of having met and talked with and learning to love Larry Trapp has been eye-opening for me. Larry has helped me realize something about my religion that I've taught a lot of people: I am obligated to try to love Larry Trapp—to hate what he stood for, but to love Larry Trapp.

Q. *Before you met Mr. Trapp, did you have any idea how extensive these racist organizations were?*

Weisser: They are larger than I might have expected. The extent of the hate network in the U.S. is frightening, and that network extends beyond our borders. The neo-Nazis are on the rise in Germany, France and other countries of Europe. The appearance of swastikas in Jewish cemeteries is again on the rise, and the destruction of Jewish-owned property is on the rise.

Q. *Mr. Trapp, what do the past few months tell you about the past few decades of your life?*

Trapp: They tell me I've got a lot of rebuilding to do. I want to try to change some minds. I know I can't change the hard-core racists, but maybe I can put something in the back of their mind that they can think about as time goes on. People who are borderline racists—maybe I can get to them before they cross that line, because once they cross that line, they get indoctrinated too heavily.

Q. *I understand that you received distressing medical news recently. Does that change any of your plans?*

Trapp: The doctor told me I have six months to a year to live. I think I can push it further, because I'm ornery as hell. At least I want to get a group started that will teach people to help one another. I'm not going to stop just because I'm sick.

Q. *You were born Roman Catholic. Do you have any interest in converting to Judaism?*

Trapp: Yes. Oh, definitely. That's my goal. I think the Jewish religion saved me. The only thing that'll keep me from converting is if there's not enough time.

Q. *Cantor Weisser, how do you feel about his converting?*

Weisser: Judaism doesn't actively seek converts, but if Larry wants to make the effort to adopt the Jewish religion, I don't think I or anybody else should put barriers in his way. I would be more than happy and, in fact, honored if Larry follows through and makes that religious affirmation.

Q. Quite a sea change.

Weisser: The whole course of Larry's history has changed. My history has changed.

Trapp: I think I was meant to be a Klansman, meant to be a Nazi, meant to do the various things I've done so I could learn that they weren't right, so that maybe, out of my experience, I can help other people change their way of thinking. I think the whole thing was planned out. I really do.

Coming Out
of Hatred

MARK FLANIGAN

In the following essay former Nazi skinhead Mark Flanigan discusses some of the reasons he became a white supremacist at the age of eighteen. Flanigan states that the economic hardships and alienation he experienced while he was growing up made him a good candidate for membership in a hate group. Such groups tend to provide easy answers to complex problems, he notes, which make them attractive to unhappy people. The passage of the Hate Crimes Prevention Act, Flanigan argues, would send a clear message to society that crimes motivated by a victim's gender, sexual orientation, or disability—as well as those motivated by racial or religious prejudice—are not to be tolerated. Flanigan is now a teacher in Arlington, Virginia, and a regular volunteer with human rights groups.

My name is Mark Flanigan, and I am a former neo-Nazi, so I speak of intolerance from an intensely personal perspective. Nearly 13 years ago, at age 18, I joined the white supremacist movement in Pittsburgh. I became a skinhead leader: organizing rallies, writing articles, and making hatred were the very center of my existence. People of color, gays and lesbians, Jewish people—they did not measure up as members of the "Aryan race," I preached, and were not worthy to share this country with the white heterosexual Christians who built it.

Although I have long since rejected that message of hate, I live each day with the grim reminder that the poisonous rhetoric I once spouted is the very same venom that manifested itself in the senseless, brutal killings of Matthew Shepard, Brandon Teena, and James Byrd Jr. It has taken me nearly

Excerpted from "Coming Out of Hatred," by Mark Flanigan, *The Advocate*, July 4, 2000. Copyright © 2000 by *The Advocate*. Reprinted with permission.

PERSONAL NARRATIVES AND PERSPECTIVES • 211

a decade—I am now age 30—to feel comfortable speaking about my past mistakes, but if my life story can change even one person's mind, that's a burden I am willing to bear.

THE MOTIVATIONS BEHIND HATE CRIMES

As a former white supremacist I understand some of the motivations behind hate crimes. Hate groups feed our natural aversion to "the unknown" by providing easy answers to complex social and political questions, and quick comfort to unhappy people. Many things led me to the white supremacist movement: my parents' divorce; shame over the economic indignities my family suffered when I was growing up; the rudderless, antisocial behavior I indulged in while in the punk rock scene. My anger was fueled by drugs and alcohol, and soon fanned into flames of hatred by neo-Nazi mentors who made me feel like a part of their movement. I was told that my hard life was part of an orchestrated anti-white conspiracy. I finally felt as though I had come "home."

Hate crimes are the very real manifestation of irrationally blaming others for our problems and disappointments in life. One powerful way to counter the rhetoric of hatred, I believe, is passage of the Hate Crimes Prevention Act, which would add crimes motivated by a victim's sex, sexual orientation, or disability to the list of hate crimes already recognized by federal law: those motivated by race, religion, color, or national origin.

Whether or not the act can somehow prevent such crimes may be open to debate, but passing this act would certainly represent a clear, unambiguous message by the federal government of support for tolerance. Without such leadership neither state and local governments nor the private sector can be expected to enforce similar policies on the street and on the job.

THE NEED FOR COALITIONS

Certainly, no group that experiences hate-motivated violence should be willfully excluded from such protections. But we have to recognize that political change is effected by coalitions. The gay, lesbian, bisexual, and transgendered community must continue to build bridges of consensus among heterosexuals of all backgrounds and races, and to flame the debate in terms that Middle America can appreciate: liberty and individual freedom.

What could be more eloquent and clear than the Declaration of Independence? All people, it says, "are created equal [and] endowed by their Creator with certain unalienable Rights . . . Life, Liberty and the Pursuit of Happiness." We must make the clear case to Middle America that legislation protecting gays and lesbians as well as other groups is not a "zero-sum" game—that is, protecting one group does not lessen the freedoms that any other American currently enjoys. To the contrary, an inclusive hate-crimes law will further validate our nation as a free government of laws, a nation that protects the rights of the individual citizen. These are not "special rights," but essential and equal protections.

In 1944 we shed our blood on the beaches of Normandy in a united effort to liberate Europe from the dark cloud of Nazism. If we truly believe in the freedom that Normandy preserved, then we must also believe that anyone's exclusion from the blessings of liberty is fundamentally inconsistent with our most cherished values. In the name of liberty, Americans of all races, religions, and sexual orientations must work together to ensure the passage of the Hate Crimes Prevention Act.

Attending the Aryan Nations Congress in Northern Idaho

RAPHAEL S. EZEKIEL

The following selection is taken from Raphael S. Ezekiel's book *The Racist Mind: Portraits of American Neo-Nazis and Klansmen*. In researching for his book Ezekiel interviewed dozens of members of militant white separatist groups and attended several of their rallies, always revealing that he was a left-wing Jewish professor who taught at the University of Michigan. His aim was to obtain a complex understanding of the lives of white racists as a means to honestly examine the nature of racism. In this excerpt, Ezekiel describes his experience listening to anti-Semitic and racist speeches at a 1989 Aryan Nations conference in Idaho.

I had met several times with Richard Butler, leader of Aryan Nations, an organization that has been one of the most influential supremacist forces, at the compound in Hayden Lake, Idaho, and had talked several times with him and his wife in Arkansas during the Fort Smith trial. [In 1988, Butler and several other members of the Aryan Nations and the Order were tried for sedition in Fort Smith, Arkansas. All of the defendants were acquitted.] Aryan Nations had quit admitting journalists to their annual summer Congress, but Butler agreed to let me come and sit in for the two-day affair the summer after Fort Smith. This took place, as the speeches imply, several years before the collapse of the Soviet Union, so details of a speech would differ today; the themes would not.

I took almost verbatim notes during the speeches; I tran-

Excerpted from *The Racist Mind: Portraits of American Neo-Nazis and Klansmen*, by Raphael S. Ezekiel (New York: Viking Penguin, 1995). Copyright © 1995 by Penguin Putnam Inc. Reprinted with permission.

scribed those notes each night. I composed the following description a bit later.

"ARYANS ONLY"

The talks begin in the middle of the morning—a few hours after I have made my drive north from the motel, have driven the country road, enjoying the crisp northern air, the conifers, the hills, but have driven with a considerable taste of apprehension in my mouth. Strong emotions alternate as I drive. I am eager and curious; the annual Aryan Nations Congress is a major event in the racist calendar nationally, and I am sure two days of observation will teach me much about the movement and its leadership ranks. I am edgy, a little afraid that I won't really be allowed in. And, finally, there is that edge of hesitation; I will be the only outsider in this secluded compound, the only non-"Aryan."

The sign at the bottom of the hill reads ARYANS ONLY; also the sign at the top, where the entry drive ends. The guards accept my explanation that the leader has invited me; they check my name on their sheet; I am waved to a meadow to park among the rows of dusty vans and pickups. Little tents dot the ground from there back to the compound proper, back to the church building which will be our auditorium, back to the wooden platform on which we are asked to stand for the flag raisings. Throughout this first hour, throughout in fact the entire weekend, the "Horst Wessel Lied" sounds from the loudspeakers in the wooden watchtower that has been constructed atop the main building. I know this song, the marching song of Hitler's party, have heard the somewhat sanitized version that is sung in English at meetings of American racists, have often heard on record or in films the German of the original, appreciate the song for its raw quality, know the opening: *Die Fahne hoch! Die Reihen fest geschlossen!*—"The flags high! The ranks tightly closed!" The song continues: *SA marschiert*—"The SA [the storm troop] marches." A similar party song, similarly popular, comes to the point: *Wenn's JudenBlut von Messer spritzt!*—"When Jew blood spurts from the knife!"

For two days the party anthem plays from the watchtower. I am filled with it. Are German marching songs truly more harsh than others, or is it my associations? Why are they so compelling? The party anthem does not cease, not even on the second day, when there are christenings and a wedding; even then this is the music at hand. It is played slowly, a dirge, at the ritual section of the program; at this slower pace it is strangely melancholy and stirring, like those other German marching songs— *Ich hat' ein' Kameraden* ... So much emotion is wrapped up in the imagery of soldiering for this culture. The sentimentality of the male world. I remember the barrenness of my two years of service. (The mess sergeant, deeply drunk, cries out to us KPs, one arm on my shoulder, the other holding the bottle high—it is Christmas night, we Jews have volunteered for this shift; it is midnight, we sit exhausted on the mess hall steps, his to torment or bore in the Georgia night; he is regular Army, over the hill, drunk, lonesome, weepy—"If only," he cries, "If only we can all be together next year!" "Yes, Sergeant," we draftees answer, thinking quietly: *God fucking forbid!*)

The world of men! The lifeless world of men only! I have worked there: the Army, prison, reform school. Now Naziland. Male bonding and other horseshit.

And here, the compound in Idaho, is a world of men. Women are present, as wives, as girlfriends, as supportive people. Women serve the meals. Men lead the rituals; men give the speeches. No woman addresses the group.

THE CEREMONIES

The ceremonies begin shortly after my arrival. I have had time only to walk about a little, noting the hand-clasping, the greetings. I nod hello to several people I have met at gatherings before. But I am one of the few who is not in a cluster of friends. Pastor Butler has us mount the wooden platform that faces the flagpoles. Butler is the founder, has created both Aryan Nations and its religious identical twin, the Church of Jesus Christ, Christian. (I have queried him a lot about the Christian Identity theology of the church, but have never dared to ask about the name—should we distinguish it from the Church of Jesus Christ, Moslem?) I am nervous, jammed among the attendees on this platform.

Pastor Butler drones an invocation. Now the Aryan Nations flag is raised as the party anthem increases in volume; everyone but me lifts an arm in the Nazi salute as the flag climbs up the pole. (We are far from my childhood: the classes lined up for the flag raising at Jim Bowie Grade School.) The Aryan Nations flag is black, red, white, a sword crossing an almost horizontal N to suggest strongly a swastika; adjacent poles support an American flag and a red Nazi flag with its grim black swastika. . . .

We enter the anteroom with its hanging flags of the Northern European nations; most of the militants in attendance use the peculiar Christian Identity religion as a major organizing tool, and Identity preaches that the true Israelites (the "Aryans") founded the Northern European nations after their expulsion from Palestine. It preaches that the Aryans are called now by their heavenly white Father to world domination, to rule over the dark subhuman races, and to a struggle to death with Satan's nonhuman children, the Jews.

The Northern European flags hang from poles mounted diagonally near the ceiling; a row of banners is achieved, most handsomely. The colors are joined by several additional flags— that of Spain, chosen perhaps for its former Fascist government; that of British Columbia, chosen as part of the new homeland to come, the Northwest; and for the same reason, the flags of Washington and Idaho. Our walk down this path of banners takes us alongside walls of Aryan Nations art, pictures drawn perhaps by prisoners and mailed in (the organization and most like it maintain a highly active correspondence with prison populations). In each drawing, a youth of Nordic bearing, a young man with high cheekbones, plunges a spear or a sword into the belly of a serpent or a dragon; each of the impaled animals is identified by a six-pointed Star of David and the hammer-and-sickle of Communism. Between two of these pictures hangs a framed, idealized portrait of the face of

Understanding Racist Voices

Author Raphael S. Ezekiel discusses his reasons for studying the lives of militant white separatists.

People sometimes ask me why I have studied these [white racist] groups. . . .The issue of race is absolutely central to American life. Our lives are deeply affected by the conceptions that segments of our society have of one another and by the institutions that have grown up over the years to embody these conceptions. It is necessary to explore these conceptions. The militant racist groups are worth studying in their own right; they have impact. But they are especially worth study because they let us see white racism in its unfiltered, unguarded form.

Adolf Hitler. He is noble and suffering; shining black hair and strong cheekbones surround deep, gleaming eyes. The intent eyes demand our attention.

We walk from the anteroom into the church itself, a hall perhaps as long as three or four ordinary garages, perhaps half that wide. Windows with a thin border of stained glass give views of the green trees, a meadow, and a hill. Up front are a banner and a lectern. The lectern, the altar, is dominated by an upright Roman sword, the symbol of the organization and its version of the Cross. This sword, this Cross, bears a swastika at its hilt. A memorial wreath to Rudolf Hess, Hitler's lieutenant who had died not long before, stands beside the altar.

THE SPEECHES

The speeches begin and run through the day. I sit quietly at first; soon take a couple of notes, in astonishment; then begin to scribble an all-but-verbatim record. The material is too dramatic to be lost, regardless of the ill will that note taking may

The history, the experiences, and the cultural lore that operate on the white racist operate on each white American; and each of us, regardless of origin, has internalized at least a part of the set of beliefs and emotions that predominate in the white racist. We who are mostly nonracist, whose minds and spirits are 70 or 80 percent nonracist, cannot act in a way that can be trusted until we have become familiar with our own inner parts that do speak in a racist voice. We need to come to know our own racism, so that it does not trip us when we are trying to behave responsibly. The energy we have spent in hiding that part of ourselves from our awareness is energy we can *use* in trustworthy acts to build coalitions.

Raphael S. Ezekiel, *The Racist Mind: Portraits of American Neo-Nazis and Klansmen,* 1995.

cause. Butler and I had made no agreement about my activities, but I had not expected or wanted to play so visible a role; all the same, the real words—more or less—mattered too much to trust to unaided memory.

The first speaker complains about the ads in his city's transport system advocating "the ultimate lifestyle," that is, the use of condoms. He attacks what he called "AIDS groups." The second speaker, a retired military man, sixtyish, round-faced, and vigorous, a stocky man with a big chest, tells us early in his talk that he had become involved in Korea before the war there, that he had been in a community that was the subject of a Communist-attempted coup. That he had seen a nun bayoneted to a wall; he had seen, he says, a baby grabbed and its head smashed against the wall. He had seen soldiers seize a baby and toss it from one to another, catching it on bayonet tips at each toss. He had seen forty beautiful young girls taken from a mission school and stripped and raped. He had seen a beautiful young woman stripped and attached to a tree by bayonets through her breasts, with a rice bowl of oil placed between her thighs and set aflame. This, he tells us, was not an isolated event; since the Russian Revolution, 140 million people had been slain "by the Jew Talmudic Communists."

Every evil, he tells us, comes from money. "And behind money is the Zionist Talmudic Jew." The Federal Reserve system, he tells us, is a private system owned by eight banks, all of them Jewish, four of them foreign; his list includes Warburg, Lazard Fréres, Rothschild, Kuhn-Loeb, and Chase Manhattan. We must get rid of the Federal Reserve system and of the income tax. We must repudiate the national debt.

"We must," he goes on, "tell the people at the top: *There will be treason trials! You will be strung from the trees!*"

The room explodes in loud applause. Cries of *"Hail Victory!"* Cries of *"White Power!"*

The immigration since 1900 has been alien, he tells us, alien in every way, not Christian. The country was not set up to be pluralistic. He tells us "nigger jokes"—jokes about "nigger preachers," "nigger churches." Americans, he notes, are lazy in their thinking, apathetic, listening to TV, but awakening, beginning to awaken to the dangers of Zionism. Back in 1902, he tells us, the international Zionists decided to destroy the four nations that must be destroyed if the Jews are to control the world: Russia, Germany, the United States, and Canada. They set aside $2 billion for that purpose, the financing coming from Jews in America. Lenin's plan is on schedule, the encirclement of the United States. In 1943, forty-seven U.S. students, forty-five of them Jews, were sent to Russian schools and came back charged to infiltrate American schools; the results, he points out, are visible in the Vietnam protests.

We need, he tells us, free enterprise, respect for the family, and the end of integration. We see around us treason. "The men behind the Iron Curtain would not be afraid to fight, those who have seen their families slaughtered by the Jew Talmudic Communists."

He recites for us much of a heroic ode by Byron, winding up at its dramatic description of one man's sacrifice: "We need men at the gap! *Who will stand at the gap with me?"*

The crowd explodes in cries of *"Hail Victory! Hail Victory! Hail Victory! White Power! White Power!"*. . .

CHRISTIAN IDENTITY

A Klan leader speaks next. He is neatly dressed, as usual, and his thin mustache is neatly trimmed. A prissy fellow, he pastors at an Identity church in the South and leads one of the largest Klans.

He asks that we join him in singing "My Country 'Tis of Thee . . ." and after we do, he asks rhetorically why there have been so many attacks at this point on the Christian Identity movement; he lists books, articles, movies. *Why* is there this hatred? There is a real war in the world, he tells us; the seed of the white race is at war with the seed of the Serpent, the Bolshevik. "We will win or we will bend our backs for all eternity." The Jew has a natural propensity to destroy the morals and the children we love, he tells us. There is eternal warfare between the offspring of the Lord and the offspring of the Serpent. "They hate us, they hate our Father, they hate our culture, they hate our music, they hate our children." They are the Antichrist, he declares. The hatred will not go away just because we ignore it; it will go on until Christ returns.

The Jews, he goes on, are a people with one goal: to destroy our faith, to destroy our children. A few years ago a survey was made of the members of the American Jewish Congress, he reports. On every question, the members responded the opposite of the traditions of our fathers—ninety percent favored abortion; ninety percent said homosexuality was okay. It was the same on gun control and on race mixing. "They are a different people that think differently from us. Their sole object is to change our form of thinking."

The children of Satan, he reports, are in rebellion against Christ. They want to change us. They hate us because we love our nation, our morals, our families. We look at what has happened in the last twenty-five or thirty years—the abortions, the homosexuality, the race mixing. We can see that the idea of the Jews is to change us; that the United States will be ruled by God or by tyrants.

We in the United States, he goes on, have joined the rebellion against God, have joined the evil empire. The average church at this time sees nothing wrong with race mixing, with homosexuality. But the Bible, he reminds us, "does not say *convert* the homos, have *dialogue* with the queers. The Bible says to *execute* them!"

Loud applause greets this statement. . . .

ANOTHER KLAN LEADER

The final seasoned speaker of the daytime program comes up, another Klan leader. He is of medium height, wears a black T-shirt and a sailor hat. He has a rugged air. His words are rough.

"I feel like a real white man here," he begins, "away from the nigger scum back where we are organizing. I have been in the Klan eight years." He lists areas in the South and in the Midwest where he has lived and organized. "We believe in the Northwest Territory; it is the only way to give our children a future away from the cesspool." If you totally trust God, he tells us, you'll see the miracles you want. He tells how he had come alone to his new location, had distributed literature, had worked at this for three or four months before making his first contacts. "One of my greatest desires," he says, "is to recruit a man like Bob Mathews or Adolf Hitler." (Mathews created the Order.)

He tells how he had tied up his town by trying to get onto the cable public access channel with the white racist videos distributed by Tom Metzger's White Aryan Resistance; the story had burst into the newspapers "on the birthday of Martin Lucifer Coon." A great hassle had ensued over issues of freedom of speech, and he still has the city tangled up. "We come across," he tells us, "as professionals. We wear our three-piece suits. We say 'Negro.' We say 'Jew.'"

It only takes two or three people to do so much, he tells us. "The sedition trial at Fort Smith put new fire in my blood. I don't know what the movement would do without Robert

Miles or Richard Butler or Louis Beam. But we would step in." Necessity would guide us. "If we can survive the traitors, the Ellisons, we are going to win." (Jim Ellison had testified against the other leaders at Fort Smith, in hopes of reducing his sentence.) "The Jews are on the run! They are panicking. They are going to go to South America.

"The people are brainwashed. It is like Farrakhan said, ninety percent of white people ninety percent of the time have their mind on their pocketbook, their mouth, or their genitals."

This man has a strong physical presence; he holds the audience. "ZOG [the Zionist Occupation Government] is coming apart at the seams!"

We preach survivalism, he tells us. Store your food, store your AK47s. We know you informers are out there, he adds, his eyes scanning the audience.

"Be careful. They will try to entrap you. Keep your weapons legal: semiautomatic. Be ready. Get ready. Move to the Northwest, you can live off this land. My fight is in my city. I love the fight! I love turning the city inside out!

"We love the white people," he continues. "There has been forty years of brainwashing, but they will come to us. And then," he thunders, "*We are going to drive these Jews out of the country! Into the sea!*" The audience erupts: "Hail Victory! White Power!"

"When I see what the Jews are doing to our people, what the Jews are doing to Germany . . . when I see what they are doing to our women—turning them into men, sending them to go to work, turning their heads—The blacks will be sent back to Africa. BUT THE JEWS? *The sword to THEM! Put tote bags on their heads!*" He finishes to thunderous applause. . . .

The speeches close, and I walk out into the slanting sun of very late afternoon. I walk about, nod to a few people, pay for a Styrofoam cup of coffee, listen a bit to conversations, and leave; I will not wander there in the dark to hear the nighttime speeches; prudence forbids. I return to the Day's Inn and spend some hours typing the notes I have scribbled all afternoon, anxious to transcribe them while my memory is fresh. . . .

TALKING WITH SKINHEADS

[The following day] I wander the meadows. I talk with Skinheads from Portland and Las Vegas. They believe everything they have heard. That they are Israelites. That Christ was white, not a Jew. That this is a Christian Republic, this is Christian Territory. God gave the Bible to us, the Christians.

On all sides, among the Skins, Klansmen, "Aryans," the word *Jew* is heard. The Jew can be an Indian, he can be anything. He is greed. The Jew is the enemy; he pushes us. The Jew is attacking, coming closer and closer. Something has to break.

I try to make estimates. Perhaps a third of the people are over fifty years old, perhaps a quarter in their twenties. About half look a little twitchy; the rest look quite ordinary. Many people are in uniforms.

As I am talking with a Skinhead by their tents, the rugged Klansman who had called for the killing of the Jews joins me. We walk off together. He asks my name. He asks whether I am religious. I assume he means am I Jewish, and assure him that I am a Jew. He knows what I am doing, he says; Butler had explained the research. I say, "That was quite a speech you gave yesterday." He agrees. I say, "It was pretty hard on the Jews, wasn't it?" He says that sometimes you get carried away. We stroll on. I explain the research further; I tell him that I would probably want to come down to his city and interview him. "Yeah, come on," he says. "You'd be welcome, Rafe."

I thank Butler and depart. I drive through foothills and prairie to Spokane; I watch cloud and conifer, hill and grass. I am dazed.

Behind me, the participants make their good-byes to one another, plan new meetings. The "Horst Wessel," presumably, continues.

A year or two later, Portland Skinheads instigated by Tom Metzger's agents have assaulted a young Ethiopian man on the street, killing him with blows to the head from a baseball bat. Between 1990 and 1993, Skinheads—courted and fed dogma by supremacist groups—kill twenty-two people, most of them nonwhites, gays, homeless, or suspected turncoats from their own ranks.

Quite recently I see the rugged Klan leader ("Yeah, come on. You'd be welcome, Rafe") on network TV news. He is in Germany, making links with the resurgent neo-Nazis who have been firebombing the homes of Turkish workers. He is showing them how to hold cross burnings.

CHRONOLOGY

April 1865
The Civil War ends with the defeat of the Confederacy.

December 24, 1865
Six former Confederate soldiers in Pulaski, Tennessee, establish a secret club which soon becomes known as the Ku Klux Klan.

April 1867
The Ku Klux Klan holds its first convention in Nashville, Tennessee. The Klan drafts a declaration of principles and Nathan Bedford Forrest is elected as the organization's first Grand Wizard.

1867–1868
The Klan grows increasingly violent, burning down southern black schools and churches and killing or injuring thousands of former slaves and their supporters.

April 20, 1871
Congress passes the Ku Klux Klan Act, which authorizes the use of the U.S. Army to control the Klan. Klan activity begins to die down.

1896
In *Plessy v. Ferguson*, the Supreme Court rules that state governments can segregate people of different races as long as "separate but equal" facilities are available.

1898
In *Williams v. Mississippi*, the Supreme Court upholds the use of literacy tests and poll taxes as a prerequisite for voting.

These requirements, applied in discriminatory ways, bar most southern blacks from voting.

1905
Thomas Dixon Jr.'s *The Clansman* is published.

1915
Large numbers of African Americans begin migrating from the South to the North. D.W. Griffith's epic pro-Klan film, *The Birth of a Nation*, is released. William Joseph Simmons establishes the Invisible Empire, Knights of the Ku Klux Klan.

1920
The *Dearborn Independent*, a Michigan newspaper owned by auto magnate Henry Ford, begins publishing a series of articles about an alleged international Jewish conspiracy to take over the world. These articles are later compiled into a book, *The International Jew*.

1925
The Klan boasts 4 million members, making it the most influential political organization in the United States. Public sentiment turns against the Klan after David Curtis Stephenson, the Grand Dragon of Indiana, is convicted of murder.

1927
Public outcry against *The International Jew* causes Henry Ford to retract the book's accusations and to close down the *Dearborn Independent*.

1929
Klan membership dwindles to less than fifty thousand.

1933
Adolf Hitler becomes chancellor of Germany. In the United States, William Dudley Pelley establishes the Silver Shirts, modeled after Hitler's Brown Shirts.

1935

In the wake of Louisiana senator Huey P. Long's assassination, his campaign manager, Gerald L.K. Smith, gains prominence. Smith influences the leadership of several white separatist groups later in the twentieth century.

1938

Charismatic radio priest Charles Coughlin encourages his followers to form a "Christian Front" to battle the "red front of Jewish-backed communism." Young Coughlinites attack Jews and Jewish-owned businesses in several eastern and midwestern cities.

1945

World War II ends. Wesley Swift founds the Church of Jesus Christ Christian in Lancaster, California.

1946

Atlanta physician Sam Green establishes the Association of Georgia Klans, the first in a series of mid-to-late-twentieth-century independent Klans.

1954

On May 17, in *Brown v. Board of Education*, the Supreme Court declares that racially segregated public education is unconstitutional. In July, anti-integrationist White Citizens' Councils start forming in the South.

1958

Robert Welch founds the John Birch Society. George Lincoln Rockwell founds the American Nazi Party (ANP).

1960

Ex–Birch Society member Robert DePugh founds the Minutemen.

1961

Klan members lead mobs attacking civil rights Freedom Riders in Alabama, prompting Attorney General Robert Kennedy to send five hundred federal marshals to the state. Subsequently, several Klan groups hold a conference in Georgia and establish the United Klans of America.

1963

In September, four black girls are killed in the bombing of the Sixteenth Street Baptist Church in Birmingham, Alabama; Klan members are among the suspects in the bombing.

1964

In August, the bodies of three civil rights workers—two white and one black—are discovered near Philadelphia, Mississippi; the Klan and local police are implicated in their deaths.

1965

In March, white civil rights worker Viola Liuzzo is shot and killed in Loundes County, Alabama, as she drives a black youth in her car; three Klansmen are eventually convicted on federal civil rights charges related to the crime and sentenced to ten years in prison.

1967

ANP leader Rockwell is assassinated.

Late 1960s

Ex–Birch Society member and ex-ANP publicist William Pierce founds the National Alliance.

1973

Richard Butler establishes Aryan Nations–Church of Jesus Christ Christian on a twenty-acre compound near Hayden Lake, Idaho. After years of FBI infiltration, Klan membership drops to a low of fifteen hundred.

1975

David Duke takes over leadership of the Knights of the Ku Klux Klan in Louisiana. Tom Metzger is ordained as a Christian Identity minister in Los Angeles, California.

1977

Klan member Robert Chambliss is convicted for murder for his participation in the 1963 church bombing that killed four black girls.

1978

William Pierce publishes *The Turner Diaries* under the pseudonym Andrew MacDonald.

1979

At an anti-Klan rally sponsored by the Communist Workers Party in Greensboro, North Carolina, five Communist activists are killed during a shootout between demonstrators and a group of both neo-Nazis and Klansmen.

1980

Duke founds the National Association for the Advancement of White People (NAAWP).

1981

Under the leadership of Grand Dragon Louis Beam, Texas Klan members burn fishing boats owned by Vietnamese immigrants to show their opposition to Vietnamese resettlement in the United States.

1982

Aryan Nations begins holding annual congresses near Hayden Lake, Idaho.

1983

Metzger founds White American Resistance, which is later renamed White Aryan Resistance (WAR). Robert Mathews establishes the Order, also know as the Silent Brotherhood.

1984

In June, Jewish radio–talk show host Alan Berg is killed by members of the Order. In December, Order leader Mathews is killed by government agents after a thirty-six-hour standoff on Whidbey Island, Washington.

1989

Duke wins a seat in the Louisiana State House of Representatives. After a jury trial, Beam and other separatists with ties to the Klan and Aryan Nations are acquitted of plotting violent strikes against the government.

1990

The Southern Poverty Law Center wins a $12.5 million lawsuit against WAR when Metzger is found liable in the 1988 skinhead murder of Ethiopian immigrant Mulugeta Seraw.

1995

In April, a bomb blast destroys the Alfred P. Murrah Federal Building in Oklahoma City, killing 168 people. Two suspects in the bombing, Terry Nichols and Timothy McVeigh, are linked to antigovernment militias. McVeigh is alleged to have been influenced by *The Turner Diaries*.

2000

Duke founds the National Organization for European American Rights (NOFEAR).

2001

Timothy McVeigh is executed for his part in the Oklahoma City bombing.

FOR FURTHER RESEARCH

Michael Barkun, *Religion and the Racist Right: The Origins of the Christian Identity Movement.* Chapel Hill: University of North Carolina Press, 1994.

Chip Berlet, ed., *Eyes Right! Challenging the Right-Wing Backlash.* Boston: South End Press, 1995.

Tyler Bridges, *The Rise of David Duke.* Jackson: University Press of Mississippi, 1994.

Howard L. Bushart, John R. Craig, and Myra Barnes, *Soldiers of God: White Supremacists and Their Holy War for America.* New York: Kensington, 1998.

David M. Chalmers, *Hooded Americanism.* New York: Franklin Watts, 1981.

Jessie Daniels, *White Lies: Race, Class, Gender, and Sexuality in White Supremacist Discourse.* New York: Routledge, 1997.

Morris Dees and Steve Fiffer, *Hate on Trial.* New York: Villard Books, 1993.

Betty A. Dobratz and Stephanie L. Shanks-Meile, *"White Power, White Pride!": The White Separatist Movement in the United States.* New York: Twayne, 1997.

Raphael S. Ezekiel, *The Racist Mind: Portraits of American Neo-Nazis and Klansmen.* New York: Viking Penguin, 1995.

Kevin Flynn and Gary Gerhardt, *The Silent Brotherhood: Inside America's Racist Underground.* New York: Free Press, 1989.

Eric Foner, *Reconstruction: America's Unfinished Revolution, 1863–1877.* New York: Harper & Row, 1988.

Mark S. Hamm, *American Skinheads: The Criminology and Control of Hate Crime.* Westport, CT: Praeger, 1993.

John Higham, *Strangers in the Land*. New Brunswick: Rutgers University Press, 1963.

Stanley F. Horn, *Invisible Empire: The Story of the Ku Klux Klan, 1866–1871*. Boston: Houghton-Mifflin, 1939.

Valerie Jenness, *Hate Crimes: New Social Movements and the Politics of Violence*. New York: Aldine de Gruyter, 1997.

Nancy MacLean, *Behind the Mask of Chivalry: The Making of the Second Ku Klux Klan*. New York: Oxford University Press, 1994.

Jack B. Moore, *Skinheads Shaved for Battle: A Cultural History of American Skinheads*. Bowling Green, OH: Bowling Green State University Popular Press, 1993.

William Peirce Randel, *The Ku Klux Klan: A Century of Infamy*. Philadelphia: Chilton Books, 1965.

Leo P. Ribuffo, *The Old Christian Right: The Protestant Far Right from the Great Depression to the Cold War*. Philadelphia: Temple University Press, 1983.

James Ridgeway, *Blood in the Face: The Ku Klux Klan, Aryan Nations, Nazi Skinheads, and the Rise of a New White Culture*. New York: Thunder's Mouth Press, 1995.

Lyman Tower Sargent, ed., *Extremism in America: A Reader*. New York: New York University Press, 1995.

William H. Schmaltz, *Hate: George Lincoln Rockwell and the American Nazi Party*. Washington, DC: Brassey's, 1999.

Southern Poverty Law Center, *The Ku Klux Klan: A History of Racism and Violence*. Montgomery, AL: SPLC, 1991.

Allen W. Trelease, *White Terror: The Ku Klux Klan Conspiracy and Southern Reconstruction*. New York: Harper & Row, 1971.

Jerome Walters, *One Aryan Nation Under God: Exposing the New Racial Extremists*. Cleveland: Pilgrim Press, 2000.

Donald I. Warren, *Radio Priest: Charles Coughlin, the Father of Hate Radio*. New York: Free Press, 1996.

INDEX

demise of
  first, 13–14, 62–63
  during 1970s and 1980s, 105, 106
  during 1990s, 107
  second, 94–95, 97–98
first, 11–13
  as controlling carpetbaggers, 49
  growth of, 46, 48
  idea of amusement in, 45–46
  organization of, 38–39
  power of the mysterious in,
    48–49
  reasons for organizing, 47
future of, 34
name origin, 37–38, 45
radical right wing, 133
renouncing, 207, 208
revival of, 14–16
  as big business, 73
  creed of, 80
  discrepancies within, 72–73
  first leader of, 66–67
  on growth of black race, 82–83
  on immigrants, 79–82
  initiation ceremony for, 67
  as lacking and suspicious of
    intellectualism, 75–76
  low membership rate in, 67–68
  new leader for, 73–74
  new managers of, 68–69
  peak of power in, 90–92
  political power and, 74–75
  presidential elections and, 92–94
  religious prejudices in, 71–72
  survival of white race and, 77–79
  true Americanism and, 69–71
sexual symbolism in, 57, 60–62
violence by
  congressional report on, 42–43
  debate on, 133
  during civil rights movement,
    24–25, 101–104
  first, 13, 39–43
  media on, 93
  vs. opposition to, 89
  sexual, 57–58
White Citizens' Councils and,
  109–10
on white supremacy, 87

white womanhood and, 58–60
Ku Klux Klan Act (1871), 13
*Ku Klux Klan Under the Searchlight,
  The* (Curry), 71
Kwan, Kuan M., 158

Lane, David, 138, 162
Last of the Mohicans (film), 177
law enforcement, 39–40, 101–104
Lear, Norman, 30
legislation
  black codes, 12
  hate crime, 31, 212–13
  against KKK, 13, 97–98
  racial desegregation, 99–100
Levin, Joe, 26
Levy, Daniel S., 205
Leydon, Sharon and Thomas,
  32–33
Liberty Lobby, 114
Lincoln, Abraham, 203
Lipset, Seymour Martin, 109
literature. *See specific titles*
Liuzzo, Viola, 24, 102–104
Locke, John G., 92
Lowe, David, 13

MacDonald, Andrew. *See* Pierce,
  William
MacKinnon, Catherine, 61
Mahon, Dennis, 133, 166
marriage, interracial, 182
Mason, James, 163–64
Mast, Blaine, 71–72
Mathews, Robert, 30, 139
McVeigh, Timothy, 31
media
  anti-Jewish campaign in, 17
  on civil rights issues, 196
  encouraging racial mixing, 176–77,
    178, 180–81
  impact on David Duke, 196–97
  on KKK, 15, 40–42, 93
  on racial equality, 195, 196
  on white separatism, 174
Metzenbaum, Howard, 183
Metzger, John, 29, 106
Metzger, Milton, 90
Metzger, Tom, 27, 29, 106